PROVENCE ON A BUDGET

PATRICK DELAFORCE

ROSTERS LTD.

Published by ROSTERS LTD.
23 Welbeck Street, London W1M 7PG
© Patrick Delaforce.
ISBN 0 948032 88 X

First Edition 1990

Every care has been taken to ensure that all the information in this
book is accurate. The author and publisher cannot accept any
responsibility for any errors that appear or their consequences.

Designed and published by ROSTERS
Typeset by JH Graphics Ltd, Reading, Berkshire.
Printed and bound in Great Britain by Cox & Wyman Ltd,
Reading, Berkshire.

CONTENTS

CHAPTER ONE:
A TASTE OF PROVENCE

Over the years my wife and I have travelled on many roads through Provence on our way to Monte Carlo and the Riviera and have visited all the most interesting towns, villages and sites. With the increasing popularity of the region, despite equally increasing prices, my publisher agreed with me that a book which not only explores the traditional Roman antiquities, the Camargue and the small hidden villages of the Vaucluse, but also advises readers of the modest and inexpensive hotels and restaurants of the region, would have a good market.

The flavour of Provence

Why do so many visitors come to Provence? Is it to savour the famous Provençal cuisine — dishes of *bouillabaisse, brandade de morue,* washed down with the warm, husky Côtes du Provence *rosé* wines? Or to view the flamingos, black bulls and white horses of the Camargue? Or to sit in the Vieux Port harbour of Marseille drinking Pastis and contemplating a visit to the Château d'If? Or to attend a summer festival at Aix, Arles, Avignon or Nîmes? I suppose the answer is a mixture of all these reasons, coloured by those gorgeous paintings by Cézanne and Van Gogh.

There is an infinite variety of scene. One chapter is entitled 'Provence-on-Sea' and describes many of the small resorts, marinas and the deep-water *calanques.* Rivers and canals meander through the powerful bleak mountain ranges of Ventoux and Luberon. The mighty Rhône (on which you can cruise on jolly *bateaux)* is the western border of Provence and the River Durance is a major tributary, rising in the Alps and thundering for 325 km to join the Rhône at Avignon.

All the Provençal painters valued the amazing colours to be seen — dark black cypress, green-silver olive trees, vines on terraces, fields of purple lavender, pine tree forests and cedars too, towering eucalyptus trees, pink Judas trees, lilac, mimosa, oleanders, pomegranates, fruit blossom and the paddy fields of the Camargue. The little villages with Romanesque churches, belfries and half-ruined châteaux, the elegant towns with plane tree boulevards, and everywhere butterflies hovering over the rosemary, thyme and myrtle bushes, were also a source of inspiration.

This is a book written to inform the first time visitor where to go, where to stay and how to do it on a modest budget. There are a few *caveats*. Try, if you can, to avoid high summer when the crowds are swamping the Roman antiquities, the mosquitoes are buzzing and the gypsies are jostling you in the Camargue. Keep your fingers crossed that the dreaded mistral wind that blows down the narrow Rhône valley so fiercely (mainly in winter) waits for your departure before arriving.

Of all the evocative sounding French regions (Auvergne, Burgundy, Gascony, Aquitaine etc), Provence conjures up to me romance (Petrach's verses, troubadours and Jacobites); colour (Van Gogh's poppies, Tavel *vin rosé*, green olives and scarlet tomatoes in the market place); inspiration (a hundred writers have been inspired by the region); cuisine (which has a chapter to itself); wine (which also has a chapter); and mystery (legends, monsters and the Camargue Romanies).

Where is Provence?

Everyone who contemplates a visit to Provence has a different idea of its boundaries. The French government has produced a rag-bag of five departments which I think is an administrative nonsense! For the purposes of this book I have omitted the French Riviera (Toulon to the Italian border). In any case, my recent book *The French Riviera on a Budget,* covered the two departments of the coastal Alpes-Maritimes and the hinterland of the Var. The true Provence, in my view, is the old original Roman Provence (i.e. Provincia). Basically, this incorporates the two departments of Bouches-du-Rhône i.e. the southern Rhône valley (which includes Marseille, Aix-en-Provence and Arles) and the hinterland department of Vaucluse (which includes Avignon, Orange, Apt, Carpentras, Cavaillon and the little Vaison-la-Romaine), plus three sneaky bits of the Gard department west of the Rhône (Nîmes, Pont-du-Gard and Aigues-Mortes).

I have included several chapters on historical aspects of Provence. After all, it was a highly civilised community 2,500 years ago! There is another on a writers' anthology, and another on the painters of Provence. At the back of the book are half a dozen really practical chapters on wines, cuisine, festivals, camp sites, buying property and packaged holidays. But the key chapter is entitled 'A Grand Tour of Provence', which my wife and I recently carried out. The ensuing four-teen chapters explore the towns and regions mentioned briefly on the Grand Tour, in rather more detail.

This book is one of a series entitled *On a Budget*. It is not for student backpackers because a car or bus is needed to visit three-quarters of the places mentioned off the beaten track. It is written for people like myself who want to explore the region but who simply cannot afford five-star hotels such as the Cité des Papes in Avignon, the Jules César in Arles, the Imperator in Nîmes or the Roy Réné in Aix!

Typical prices

Although France has roughly the same amount of inflationary pressures as the UK, hoteliers in France have to conform to local council rules on room charges and are in a fiercely competitive market for meal prices. Can you imagine anywhere else in the world where you can get a *decent* three course meal for 50 francs — about a fiver? Hundreds of little restaurants and hotel-restaurants offer just that, with a *pichet* of local wine, *vin de patron*, at equally benevolent prices. The only sneaky price break-out has occurred with breakfast, *petit déjeuner*, charges. A few years back they were usually in the 12–15 francs region but now are 20–25 francs per head for the usual fresh bread *(baguette)*, a croissant, lots of coffee (possibly with an acorn flavour) and plastic-wrapped jam and butter. If you are lucky you may encounter a pot of fresh butter and a pot of fresh jam, but alas, these are now rare. So, the modern day traveller's budget for two people will be about 400–500 francs per day *per couple*.

	Francs
1. Hotel room	110–130
2. Two *petits déjeuners*	35–40
3. Two evening meals *prix fixe*	100–120
4. A *pichet* of local wine	20–30
5. A day's petrol (50 – 75kms)	30–40
6. Visits to châteaux, abbeys, museums	30 – 40
7. Lunch: supermarket ham, cheese, pâté, salad, bread, butter, local wine	50–60
8. Coffee, aperitifs or soft drinks	25–30
	400–490

Of course, it is always a matter of your taste and your requirements, plus a dash of luck, whether this budget is exceeded or not. If, instead of a *pichet* (see 4 above), you choose a delicious vintage 1985 from Gigondas, then you must revise the budget!

Travel checklist

Obviously you must make sure your passport is valid and up to date, your favourite ferry company is not on strike and your tickets are accurate (correct days and times and destinations). You will, I hope, have not only purchased a Green Card for your car but have obtained some truly comprehensive insurance for all travellers accompanying you. It is far better to spend a few more pounds and, if anything, over-insure your family and all your belongings. Choosing between cash, credit cards, Eurocheques, travellers cheques or what have you, has so many pros and cos. I am a Eurocheque fan, but other people swear by Visa, Access or Barclaycard. The

Michelin map you need is No. 246, or 81/83/84, and can easily be purchased in the UK. Pack some soap too as many modest French hotels are reluctant to provide any!

The choice of route is usually between the fast autoroutes (all *péages* i.e. quite expensive tolls) but naturally very quick, and the more direct *routes nationales,* or local roads, which are cheaper and usually more interesting but may need map-reading through the towns on the way. It depends on time available for the journey, whether there are any interesting detours *en route* and the map reading skills of your family. Whatever you do, keep away from the Paris peripheric ring road in the four rush-hour periods 8.00 a.m.–9.00 a.m., 11.45 a.m.–12.15 p.m. (lunch time), 1.45 p.m.–2.15 p.m. (return from lunch) and 6.00 p.m.–7.00 p.m. (office closing times).

Hotel bookings

A few days in advance, our family tend to make a telephone reservation for the first night of the holiday, giving us some leeway for arrival. Aim to arrive before 8.00 p.m. as Madame will be getting apprehensive in her kitchen if you are any later. Many provincial restaurants serve the evening meal from 7.00 p.m. (and lunch from noon).

Hotel prices

Hotel rooms are priced per room irrespective of whether it is for one or two people. The price is posted in the entrance lobby and behind the room door. Madame will endeavour to offer you the most expensive room she has not yet 'sold' for the night. Be firm, look at the room list and ask for a room to suit your budget, and then ask to see it before making a decision. This is normal practice and Madame will expect it. Check that the room offered you is not on the noisiest side overlooking route N7 and preferably not immediately next door to the W.C.

Although the local police no longer need to examine your passport when you check in at your hotel, you may occasionally be asked to leave your passport, theoretically for the *gendarmerie*. Madame is in fact taking precautions that you do not slip away early in the morning without paying. Just smile and remember to collect it at breakfast when you pay the bill. Incidentally, all the charges on the bill are net, i.e. *servis compris* – room, breakfast, supper, wine. There is no need to add anything more unless the service has been beyond the call of duty. If you telephone from the hotel you will be billed a premium charge. Far better to do it from the local PTT or from a *Cabine de Poste*. Cheap rates are 9.30 p.m. to 8.00 a.m. Monday to Friday, after 2.00 p.m. on Saturdays, and all day on Sundays and public holidays.

To ring the UK from France from a phonebox feed in, say, 10 francs as credit, dial 19, wait for the tone to change, dial 44 then the STD number (minus the first 0), then your number. You can receive calls in the box and the number is clearly marked. To phone France from the UK dial 010 33, then the eight-figure provincial number.

Restaurants

Experienced menu-spotters, having arrived at 6.00 p.m. and parked in the main square, often select their hotel by the quality of the dinner promised for that evening. If *rognons de veau au Côtes de Provence* is on the menu and the hotel looks reasonable, that place would get my casting vote. Of course, difficulties always arise if you have, say, four vociferous members of the family with differing tastes. If by any chance the *prixfixe* menu is not handed to you by the waiter or Madame, politely but firmly ask for it. The *plat du jour* is the chef's speciality of the day and should be well-cooked, interesting and inexpensive.

If the wine list looks too expensive and daunting, ask for a *pichet* or carafe of *vin rouge/blanc/rosé du maison* which will appear rapidly at a fraction of the price of a Côte du Rhône.

Electricity

Electricity is 220 volts, so an adaptor for a hairdryer or shaver is necessary with a 2-pin plug. If you are a keen reader and do not fancy French TV in the bar in the evening, take a portable lamp with a 100 watt bulb with you. The hoteliers' thrift extends from lack of soap to very low-powered electric light bulbs!

Illness

If any member of your family has a relatively minor problem, the *pharmacie* with a green cross will have a qualified chemist who may be able to proffer treatment and will certainly know the address of the local doctor.

Driving

Remember to drive on the right, and be prudent at crossroads, roundabouts and when coming out of a petrol station. Speed limits are clearly marked on all roads in kilometres per hour. Minor roads are 90 km, dual carriageways 110 km and motorways 130 km per hour. Try to make your really long journeys on a Sunday when lorries are forbidden.

And the best time of year to go?

The winter is for the brave if the dreaded mistral wind is blowing fiercely down the Rhône valley. I have asked the locals if they can predict when it will come. A Gallic shrug of the shoulders is the answer. But lovers quarrel, families disintegrate, animals hide, and for a day or so very primitive nature rules the road, so beware! But winter *sans* mistral can be delightful. Midsummer is ideal for the young who can face the competitive crowds in the great music festivals. The hotels are full. The campsites are full. The roads are clogged. The beaches are unbearable. So my choice is for late spring, early autumn, early summer (i.e. June) and late autumn — in that order of preference.

The annual temperature guide to Provence is shown overleaf in °C

J	F	M	A	M	J	J	A	S	O	N	D
12.2	11.9	14.2	18.5	20.8	26.6	28.1	28.4	25.2	22.1	16.8	14.1

Look for the purple Judas trees, the pink tamarisks, the violet wisteria and irises and the empty roads of spring!

So, bon voyage!

CHAPTER TWO:
A GRAND TOUR

For first-time visitors to Provence I have devised a two-week Grand Tour, travelling by car and taking in all the key sights. My wife and I recently made this same tour in ten days, but it meant skimping in some places. For instance, we spent one day only in the Camargue (through which we have travelled on many previous occasions) — ornithologists can spend a week there quite happily. In the various wine regions we visited the leading wine co-operatives and tasted (again) their wines (and bought several cases), but it was a cursory look and did not do justice to the immense variety of wine regions. We looked at all the major Roman sites — as tourists, not as historians or 'antiquarians'! We visited most of the leading museums but did not, as art-historians, track down all the backgrounds that Van Gogh and Cézanne put so richly on to canvas. We visited a few of the many beaches but spent no time bathing, although in late spring/early summer we could have done. We did not climb on foot the splendid mountain ranges of Ventoux and Luberon, nor follow the Grande Randonnée trails (GR4 and GR91); one could spend a week or more doing just that. So really two weeks is just about right! Half a dozen towns make excellent bases for local regional tours and these are mentioned in this chapter. I have briefly sketched in the key visits, which are covered in more detail later on in this book in the same sequence.

On the map the Provence region is a large rectangle roughly 60 km at the north (Bollène-Vaison), about 100 km in depth (north—south) and about 110 km in width along the coastline (Cassis—Aigues-Mortes), so that daily motoring distances are likely to be of not more than 2—3 hours' duration.

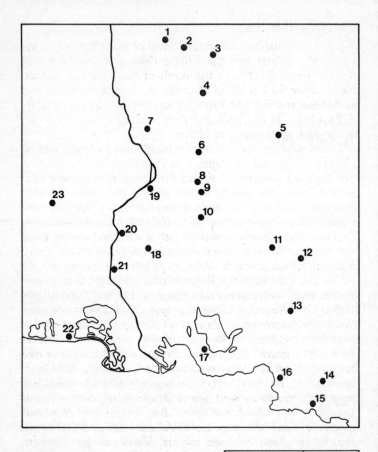

1 Gragnan	**13** Aix
2 Valréas	**14** Aubagne
3 Nyons	**15** Cassis
4 Vaison	**16** Marseille
5 Sault	**17** Martigues
6 Carpentras	**18** Les Baux
7 Orange	**19** Avignon
8 Fontaine de Valluse	**20** Tarascon
9 L'Isle-sur-la-Sorgue	**21** Arles
10 Cavaillon	**22** Stes Maries-de-la-Mer
11 Cadanet	**23** Nîmes
12 Pertuis	

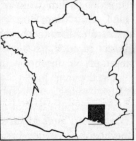

Starting the tour

Since most travellers will enter Provence from the north, via Lyon, Montélimar and the Rhône valley, the tour starts at Valréas (pop. 8,800), in the north of the Vaucluse department, some 40 km SE of Montélimar. Eventually it will end at Bollène and Pont-St Esprit 40 km SW of Valréas. Visitors to Provence arriving from the west on the Autoroute A9 can easily pick up the tour at Nîmes.

This is wine country, as shown by the names of the nearby villages of Rousset-les-Vignes, St Pantaleon-les-Vignes, and the illogical Vinsobres. It is also the centre for lavender production, and the purple fields extend for acres around. However, the main money spinner is the cardboard box industry. The Romanesque cathedral, the fourteenth-century Castle Simiane (partly now the *hôtel de ville*) and the old town with its picturesque arcade *soustets* is well worth a visit. There is a major wine co-op in Valréas. A splendid festival is held on 23 June, St John the Baptist's day, called 'Petit St Jean', and lavender processions take place on the first Sunday and Monday in August. A popular town with the fourteenth-century Avignon popes, Valréas is known as the 'Enclave des Papes' and celebrated as such in the mid-summer festival 'Nuits de l'enclave'. For a good place to stay in the plane tree boulevards, try the hotel-restaurant la Camargue, 49 Cours Jean-Jaurès, tel. 90-35-01-51, where the 55-franc menu has *lapin à la moutarde* and *gratin dauphinoise,* or the hotel-restaurant des Gourmets which has a four-course menu, unbelievably for 38 francs. Local Valréas lamb and truffles are also to be tasted on their menus. Visits can be made to Grignan (9 km west on D941) where Madame de Sévigné lived. See there the eleventh-century castle and sixteenth-century collegiate church, and visit Nyons in the valley at the River Eygues (seventh-century Saracen watchtower and arcaded old town).

Vaison-la-Romaine

Travel via Visan (pop. 1,200), south on the D976, which has the co-op Cave les Coteaux opposite the hotel-restaurant du

Midi, Ave. des Alliés, to St Maurice-sur-Eygues, and SE on D20 and D975 to Vaison-la-Romaine (pop. 5,200) where you should stay for a night. Bisected by the River Ouvèze, the town has a multitude of well-laid out Roman antiquities including a theatre, a well used bridge over the river, houses (Messii and Puymin), baths, mosaics and porticoes for which guided tours are available. On the east bank is a twelfth-century castle on a steep hill overlooking a medieval township. On the south side is the Cathedral of Notre-Dame, part sixth- to thirteenth-century with cloister and twelfth-century Chapel of St Quentin. Vaison is crammed full of tourists in season and so it is difficult to see the Roman antiquities. Try the Hôtel les Voconces, Place Montfort, tel. 90-36-00-94 where the 49-franc menu includes *salade camarguaise, filet de loup à la crème et aux fines herbes.* Excursions are NE to Puymeras (wines), west to Rasteau (wine co-op), east along the valley of the Ouvèze and walks in the Mont Ventoux range of mountains to the observatory at a height of 2,000 metres. Also to Malaucène (pop. 2,000) 10 km SE, with Pope Clement's fourteenth-century church and belfry.

Carpentras

The 30-km run SW on the D977 and D8/D7 to Carpentras takes in an intriguing selection of villages. Seguret on a hillside is one of the prettiest in Provence, with views west over the plain and a craft centre particularly noted for the clay biblical figures called *santons*. Sablet is just as pretty, with seven towers, ramparts and wine co-op. Next come two of the best quality wine villages in France — Gigondas and neighbouring Vacqueyras (see Chapter 22). You should make a stop at the wine co-op at the latter — a delightful experience — where we bought half a dozen different red wines. Just 3½ km SE on the east side of the road is the celebrated ninth-century little church Notre-Dame-d'Aubune, just before you come into Beaumes-de-Venise (pop. 1,600), celebrated for its liqueur wines (taste at co-op). Next, go 8 km into Carpentras (pop. 24,250), a large fruit and vegetable market town noted for its superb seventeenth-century synagogue, its Inguimbertine library (the finest in Provence), St Siffrein Cathedral, Roman triumphal Orange Gate and the manufacture of Berlingot sweeties! From 14 July to 15 August Carpentras hosts a major art festival. Try the Hôtel le Cours, tel. 90-63-10-07, Bd. A. Durand or the neighbouring Hôtel le Théâtre, tel. 90-63-02-90, and take your evening meal at L'Univers, Place A. Briand, two minutes' walk away. Their 49-franc menu is excellent value. A good excursion eastwards on the D942 via Mazan takes you through the gorges of the River Nesque — quite spectacular — to Sault (pop. 1,25O), a health resort with castles, medieval streets and houses. Pernes-les-Fontaines (pop. 6,000), 6 km due south on the D938, is criss-crossed with streams and canals. Ramparts, towers, fortified gates and, of course, fountains make Pernes an interesting and photogenic stop.

L'Isle-sur-la-Sorgue

Then drive south for 17 km to L'Isle-sur-la-Sorgue (pop. 12,000) known as the 'Comtaline Venice' (after the fourteenth-century Papal-owned Comtat Venaissin). Water wheels, rivers, streams, and canals provide natural power to make quilts and rugs. Look at the frescoes by Mignard and Parrocel in the seventeenth-century church. The Sorgue festival is held throughout July, and includes horse races and international motorcycle cross country championships. Amongst the plane tree esplanades are the Hôtel le Vieux Isle, 15 Rue Danton, tel. 90-38-00-46, and Hôtel Le Glacier, 7 Ave. de la Libération, tel. 90-38-08-07. The 53-franc menu at the restaurant Oustalet has *estoufade de boeuf provençale* and *brioche à la saucisse*. There are excursions from L'Isle-sur-la-Sorgue to the Grotto of Thouzon and the little town of Le Thor, 6 km to the west.

Fontaine-de-Vaucluse

Five km east is Fontaine-de-Vaucluse, where the River Sorgue surges out of a huge subterranean cave made famous by Petrarch's compositions to his unknown Laura (366 poems in the period 1337–53). Next there is a visit to the beautiful peaceful abbey, built in 1148, of Senanque (where I studied their ecclesiastic foundation chart), the unique seventeenth-century village of Les Bories (thirty restored semi-nomadic dry stone shepherd's houses shaped like Hovis loaves), the superb village of Gordes (pop. 1,600) overlooking the Vaucluse plains and Imergue River. This is the most spectacular 'village perché' in Provence, highly photogenic with a twelfth-century fortress/Renaissance château (as well as the incongruous modern Vasarely Museum). Tourists flock here in season and the hotels are relatively expensive.

Roussillon

Four km due east lies Roussillon (pop. 1,100), an ochre-coloured village with picturesque streets with artisans and artistic communities. Try the Hôtel des Ocres, Route des Gordes, tel. 90-75-60-50. Then go east via the D4 and N100 into Apt (pop. 11,300), which is on the River Calavon. It is an ideal place to explore the mountain plateau de Vaucluse to the north or the Montagne de Luberon to the south. Apt is noted for its ochre mines and refining, its lavender culti-vation, truffles and preserved fruits and candies. They have been making sweets here since 1365. Look at the clock tower and crypts of St Anne's Cathedral. Try the Hôtel de Palais, 12 Place Gabriel-Peri, tel. 90-74-23-54 or Le Relais de Roquefure, tel. 90-74-22-80.

From Apt, we head south on the D943 to visit the fifteenth-century château of Lourmarin, through the Combe or pass of that name which bisects the Regional Park of Luberon (250,000 acres from Cavaillon in the west to Vitrolles in the east). Next go to Cadenet (pop. 2,500), a fruit producing town (cherries and asparagus) with fortified church and ruined eleventh-century castle, and the Cistercian abbey of Silvacane built in 1144, now well restored. Follow the valley of the River Durance east to Pertuis (pop. 12,500) on the bank of the River Lèze. There are thirteenth- and fourteenth-century buildings to be seen, towers, a castle and church. There are two modest hotels, des Cornarel, 24 Rue de la Tour, tel. 90-79-14-34 and du Cours, 100 Place Jean-Jaurès, tel. 90-79-00-68.

Aix-en-Provence

From Pertuis, drive south on the D556 to Aix-en-Provence (pop. 125,000), which is one of the most elegant cities in France. In brief what you must see are: the historic Cour Mirabeau (seventeenth-century town houses, smart restaurants, cafés and shops); the fourteenth-century Cathedral of St Sauveur; the old town; the Granet Museum (portrait of Sir Thomas More, Rembrandts, Rubens and Ingres); the Tapestry Museum; the Casino; Paul Cézanne studios; the thermal spa baths in the Cours Sextius, plus dozens of other attractions. See how many of the 21 beautiful fountains you can find. Parking is predictably difficult but drive slowly round the périphérique (Bd. du Roi Réné, Bd. Carnot and Cours St Louis) until you see a vacant slot. The English have been coming to Aix since the sixteenth-century and often stayed for months on the Grand Tour. Some visitors, including Jacobite exiles, took up residence. The food is good and try the vin de Palette, a dessert wine grown in vineyards 5 km to the east of Aix. Modest hotels include the Sully, 69 Bd. Carnot, tel. 42-33-11-77; Paul, 10 Ave. Pasteur, tel. 42-23-23-89; Pax, 20 Rue Espariat, tel. 42-26-24-79 and des 4 Dauphins, 54 Rue Roux-Alpheron (being renovated), tel. 42-38-16-39. None have restaurants so try Le Terminus on the Cours Mirabeau where the 50-franc menu has *brochette à la provençale* with *pâté de sanglier* to start with. We supped well at La Grille, 18 Rue Portalis, with *daube provençale* and local *tapenade* (olive paste, herbs and capers). Try too La Grange in Carriero de Nazaret off the Cours Mirabeau, near the famous La Belle Epoque café. I have visited all of the spa towns in France — Vichy, Vittel etc — but Aix is in a class of its own, sparkling, full of fun. Try to stay a minimum of two days. In mid-summer, see the international Music Festival.

La Ciotat

From Aix drive SE on the Autoroute A8, then A52 south to
Aubagne (pop. 39,000), home of the Foreign Legion, and
continue south on the A50 to visit La Ciotat (pop. 31,800),
once a Roman port and still employing 6,000 people building
and repairing ships. To the west is the old port and to the east
La Ciotat-Plage (3 km) and Marina with man-made beaches.
The Mediterranean gleams blue and green, and Provençal
restaurants beckon with crab and *bouillabaisse*. Modest hotels
include La Marine, 1 Ave. Fernand-Gassion, tel. 42-08-35-11;
Beaurivage, 1 Bd. Beaurivage, tel. 42-83-09-68 and the
Plaisance, 15 Ave. Franklin-Roosevelt, tel. 42-83-10-19.

Cassis

Take the coast road called the Corniche des Crêtes, west
along the clifftops to Cassis (pop. 6,500) — such a charming,
pretty fishing port that it became the summer resort of painters
— Matisse, my favourite Dufy, Derain and Vlaminck. The
three beaches adjoin the Promenade des Lombards. Boats sail
frequently from the Vieux Port to the dozen *calanques* (the
deep sea creeks or fiords between Cassis and Marseille),
including En-Vau, Port-Pin and Port Miou, and to the small
islands of Cap Croisette. Cassis is now a smart resort town
and not cheap, but try the Auberge du Joli Bois, tel.
42-01-02-68 or Le Provençal, 7 Ave. Victor Hugo, tel.
42-01-72-13. St Peter's day on 29 June sees regattas and
much jollity on shore. Try the strong green-white Cassis wine
grown locally and the Provençal dishes at El Sol, 23 Quai des
Boux. The Municipal Casino is new and luxurious, open daily
3.00 p.m. to 2.00 a.m.

Marseille

From Cassis drive on the D559 for 22 km parallel to the
Mediterranean but inland into the eastern outskirts of Marseille
(pop. 880,000), the major port and second city of France. I
do not recommend staying here for too long. It is a tough
competitive city, but visit the Vieux Port, the grand Basilica
of Notre-Dame-de-la-Garde, the two adjacent cathedrals, the

main street called La Canebière and Dumas' Château d'If
(prison of the Man in the Iron Mask or 'Count of Monte
Cristo') which can all be seen in a day. Marseille boasts several
high class museums — the Maritime (closed Tuesday), Roman
Docks, Old Marseille and Historical Museum — all of which
will take another day. Le Corbusier's startling township, built
in 1957, called La Cité Radieuse, of 17 stories, is on the Bd.
Michele SE of the Vieux Port. On 15 August a pilgrimage
takes place at Bonne Mère (the local name for the Basilica of
Notre-Dame). Marseille has always traded with North Africa
and the *pieds noirs* made their home here. Take extra security
precautions in this city, empty your car and lock it firmly.
Although not typical of Provence, you should visit Marseille
as part of the Grand Tour since it is the capital of Provence-
Côte d'Azur, and the oldest town in France. There are sixty
one-star hotels and the Edmond-Rostand, 31 Rue Dragon,
tel. 91-37-74-95; Azur, 24 Cours F. Roosevelt, tel.
91-42-74-38; and the hotel-restaurant St Charles, 26 Rue
Breteuil, tel. 91-37-78-86 are reasonable and clean! Ask the
Tourist Office at 4 La Canebière near the Vieux Port for
advice and booking facilities. Try the *bouillabaisse* at
Restaurant Rascasse-Dauphin, 6 Quai de Rive-Neuve near the
old port or Chez Soi, 5 Rue Papère in the centre of town —
both good and modestly priced.

The Etang de Berre

Driving out of Marseille needs a bit of planning. You need to
go north through the docks signed for Estaque (and *not* the
Autoroute A7 to Salon) to the N568, D5 and D9 west along
the coast via several little resorts (Carry-le-Rouet and Sausset-
les-Pins) towards Martigues (pop. 42,000) which is a curious
hotch-potch of ancient and modern. The Autoroute A53 and
D5 in parallel cross over the Canal de Caronte which leads
into the large inland Etang de Berre. Called La Venise
Provençale, the old fishing and painting town with the canal
St Sebastien still retains much charm. On the first Saturday
in July there is a festival of Venetian floats and fireworks.
There are beaches nearby and many regattas. But the oil

tankers, oil reservoirs and refineries provide an incongruous background. The petrol port of Lavéra is now the largest in Europe. However, I must be charitable. The last time we were driving on the D5 to Istres parallel with the Etang we saw a huge V-shaped wedge of rosy pink flamingos — perhaps 60 or 70 — flying in perfect formation about 300 feet above the lagoon. A beautiful greeting to the Camargue. One can stay in Martigues at Le Provençal, 35 Bd. du 14 Juillet, tel. 42-80-49-16, or in Istres (pop. 30,400) 15 km NW of Martigues at the L'Escale, Bd. Quizonnier, tel. 42-55-01-88, where we had the best breakfast in Provence (French breakfasts tend to be basic and monotonous — but not at L'Escale). We also had an excellent meal at the Hôtel de France, 33 Ave. Helène-Boucher, tel. 42-55-00-02. The town has a marina on the Etang de Berre and its own private Etang de l'Olivier. We decided to miss out Salon (pop. 36,000) 24 km NE for various reasons. It is worth a visit to see the old town, the Emperi Castle, two medieval churches and Army museum. It has several budget hotels including Le Paris, Acceuil Provençal and Le Provence, but we had visited the town a dozen or more times before. It is a dog-leg away from the Camargue and the route by the N113 west of Salon towards Arles is boring and undistinguished — salt mines, bullrushes and swamps!

So, I suggest from Istres or Martigues head SW or west to the N568, and travel through the salt marshes of the Plaine de la Crau across the Canal de Marseille, past some awful oil refineries, via Port St Louis to cross the River Rhône by ferry boat at Bac de Barcarin. It costs 24 francs per car but it is the best way into the Camargue from the SE. Find the country roads D36 c and b (west of the D36) and gently meander close and parallel to the Etang de Vaccares to Méjanes to watch the cowboys (or ride a horse), looking out for birds of all kinds and shapes. On the way there is a small vineyard at Villeneuve which proves that properly nourished vines will grow in sandy soil. I have written in more detail in a later chapter about the Camargue. At the end of the D570 is Les Sts Maries-de-la-Mer with beaches, an intriguing dark church full of legends and many importunate gypsies. The ornithological park, the Museum Boumian and on the return trip north, 8 km SW of Arles, the folklore museum in the Mas du Pont de Rousty, should be seen. And boat tours of Camargue from Le Tiki, tel. 90-97-81-68, are fun.

On to Arles

Arles (pop. 50,000) is one of the five key towns of Provence. On the east bank of the Rhône, Arles was once a Greek port in the sixth century bc, and was also the crossroads between Spain and Italy. The Roman remains − a superb amphitheatre, Roman baths and theatre − the cathedral and cloisters of St Trophime and three excellent museums, make this ramparted town a delight in which to stay a day or two. Three more bonuses are looking for Van Gogh's painting sites (he painted over 300 canvases here), a visit to Frédéric Mistral's Museum Arlaten to see every detail of bygone Provençal life − a fascinating display − and finally the macabre Alyscamps, a famous Roman necropolis in walking distance from the Bd. des Lices near the Canal de Craponne. For three hundred years the visitors on the Grand Tour *had* to visit Alyscamps (in addition to the amphitheatre and arena). Arles offers delightful boat cruises on the Rhône and riverside walks. We stayed at the Terminus et Van Gogh Hotel, 5 Place Lamartine, tel. 90-96-12-32. There are two more modest hotels nearby in the Place Voltaire. Le Rhône is at No. 11, tel. 90-96-43-70 and the Voltaire at No. l, tel. 90-96-13-58. There are several good-value restaurants including Le Galoubet, 18 Rue Dr Fanton, near the Place du Forum and Le Magali in Rue Chavary. On 1 May is the feast of St George, patron saint of the Camargue *gardiens,* and the wine harvest festival and corrida (bullfight) is in late September. So Arles is an essential visit but preferably not in July/August.

North to Tarascon

Start early for the next lap! Head north to Tarascon and you will find five 'antiquities' *en route.* Initially on N570 then D17 NE to the tenth-century Benedictine abbey of Montmajour, now mainly restored; a few km further on to see Daudet's

Windmill among the pinewoods, a ten-minute walk up the slopes in Fontvielle. Next go east and north on the D5 to Les Baux-de-Provence, the exquisite hilltop village of the great lords of Baux. From its ramparts think of the twelfth-century troubadours serenading at the Court of Love. The churches, gates and the deserted village make Les Baux a vital visit (but do your homework first! I had never before heard of the warrior tribe of Baux who ruled much of the south of France in the eleventh and twelfth centuries). Again, visit out of season. Then, still on the D5, are the two lonely Roman 'Les Antiques' by the side of the road and opposite the ruins of Glanum, probably the most important archaeological site in southern France. Finally, make for St Rémy-de-Provence (pop. 8,500). This little town is a good base from which to explore the region, being almost equidistant from Arles, Tarascon and Avignon and on the doorstep of Glanum, Les Antiques, Les Baux and the Alpilles mountains. The town has two museums, the Sade family house (not *the* sadist), and Van Gogh painted 150 paintings here in his last year of life in an asylum. There are several modest hotels: La Caume, Route d'Orgon, tel. 90-92-09-40; Provence, 36 Bd. Victor Hugo, tel. 90-92-06-27; Villa Glanum, 46 Ave. Van Gogh, tel. 90-92-03-59; and Villa Verte, Ave. Fauconnet, tel. 90-92-06-14.

On to Avignon

Now head west on the D99 to Tarascon (pop. 11,000), which is twinned across the Rhône with Beaucaire (pop. 13,000). For seven centuries the great castles have been glaring at each other across the river. (Both have guided tours, closed Tuesday.) A town full of legends (festival last Sunday in June), Tarascon makes a calm base for many excursions. Budget hotels include Du Pont, 2 Ave. de la République, tel. 90-01-39-24 and Du Rhône, Place Colonel Berrurer, tel. 90-91-03-35. Walk across the bridge over the Rhône into neighbouring Beaucaire to see their castle!

Now go north on the D81 to the Abbey of St Michel-de-Frigolet, a peaceful tenth-century Benedictine retreat with a small museum and guided tours. It is a beautiful complex of buildings off the beaten track in the woods and you can have a modest meal there if you arrive at the appropriate hour. Then via Barbentane (pop. 3,300) with its fourteenth-century castle, towers and gateways, linking up with the N570 back into the Vaucluse department and into the suburbs of Avignon (pop. 91,500).

The famous St Benezet Bridge, which was completed in 1190, fortified in the fifteenth century and now has only four of the original twenty-two arches surviving, looks a little disappointing. The narrow bridge was never wide enough for dancing, but perhaps *'sur le pont d'Avignon, on y danse, tous en rond'* took place on the bridge piers? By 1376 — and the Popes settled here in 1309 — there were no less than 31 Cardinal's palaces in Avignon and the mighty Palace of the Popes, despite many vicissitudes in the French Revolution, is still one of *the* wonders of France. A visit takes two hours, costs about 21 francs and is well worth it. The views from the gardens of the Petit Palais and Rocher des Doms, of the Palace, town and the Rhône, are superb. Allow a complete day to see all that Avignon has to offer, including the Calvet Museum, cathedral and churches of St Didier and St Pierre, which are all within easy walking distance of each other. Try to avoid mid-summer even though the theatre-festival in the Popes' Palace takes place then. I discovered three modest hotels in a quiet street, Rue Agricol-Perdiguier, which is near a park and the tourist office (and regional wine office), off the main Rue de la République. The hotels are The Splendid, No. 17, tel. 90-86-14-46; the Du Parc, No. 18, tel. 90-82-71-55; and the Pacific at No. 7.

Some of the best excursions from Avignon are made by boat up or down the Rhône and Durance rivers. Consult Grands Bateaux de Provence, Allées de l'Oulle, tel. 90-85-62-25.

Heading north to Orange

Next head north on the D225, N7 to Sorgues and D17 to Châteauneuf-du-Pape (pop. 2,000), passing many well known vineyards. Here you can taste and buy at the Maison du Vin any or all of the 36 main producers' wines. The Popes' castle on the hill overlooking the small town was burnt predictably by the Germans in the Second World War, but from the remains there is a marvellous view of the Rhône valley and Avignon. Now go 10 km north on the D976 into Orange (pop. 27,500) which has two major Roman antiquities – the theatre, which can hold 12,000 people, and the commemorative triple-arched triumphal gateway on the N7 north of the town. Orange, with its distant royal links with Holland and England, is a good base from which to visit the many wine regions and Pont-St Esprit and Bollène to the NW. In Orange small hotels include des Arts, Cours Pourtoules, tel. 90-34-01-88; Lou Coudoules in Ave. de Verdun, tel. 90-34-04-14; and Le Père Tranquille, 8 Place aux Herbes, tel. 90-34-09-23. In the pedestrian centre next to the *fromagerie* La Populaire is La Sangria restaurant, with a 53-franc menu including wine.

On to Nîmes

The visitor on the Grand Tour now has a choice – to continue north and out of Provence towards Montélimar, or preferably to go SW to the incredible Roman Pont-du-Gard via the wine regions of Lirac and Tavel (reported to be the best *vin rosé* in France). Thence into Nîmes (pop. 130,000), prefecture town of the Gard to see the Roman sites (arena now used for bullfights and jazz concerts), the Maison Carrée overlooking the forum and the gardens of La Fontaine and Tour Magne. Try the hotel-restaurant Concorde, Rue des Chapeliers, tel. 66-67-91-03 or the Majestic, 10 Rue Pradier, tel. 66-29-24-14 or the Forum, Rue Trelys, tel. 66-21-74-84. We had our car burgled in Nîmes so be careful, but the food is good! Try *brandade de morue,* a cod purée. To summarise the Grand Tour, my views are as follows:

The most elegant, cosmopolitan town	Aix
The most attractive port/old harbour	Marseilles
The best seaside resort	Cassis
The best beaches	La Ciotat
The most interesting church	St Vincent at Les Baux
The best kept villages	Gordes or Seguret
The best Roman sites	Pont-du-Gard/Orange theatre/Les Antiques
The most interesting museum	The Arlaten in Arles (Frédéric Mistral)
The most attractive abbeys	St Michel-de-Frigolet and Senanques
The best wine co-op to visit	Vacqueyras
The most spectacular buildings	Palais des Papes at Avignon
The wildlife centre	The Camargue
The best meals (very subjective)	Aix, Arles and Istres
Our favourite town	Arles
The best walks	Along the Mont Ventoux range

Again — bon voyage, bonne route, bonne chance!

29

CHAPTER THREE:
HISTORICAL BRIEFING

Prehistory in Provence

Provence is not particularly rich in prehistoric finds compared, say, to the Dordogne. The skull of Grimaldi, c. 30,000 BC was found near the Italian frontier at Menton − not really in Provence! But palaeolithic caves have been identified in the cliff of Moulin-Clos, south of Apt, at Robion, near Carpentras, at St Chamas, NW of Marseille, at St Saturnin and Auribeau. (Many of the very old caves discovered were not occupied by prehistoric man. Many of these, called Avens or Balmes, at up to depths of 500 metres have been discovered in the Albion plateau north of Apt. The Loubière caves and those of Thouzon near Le Thor] offer guided tours throughout the year.

Other prehistoric sites in the Bouches-du-Rhône department are the important troglodyte grottoes at Calès, near Lamanon, the oppidum of Entremont near Aix, another at Nages near Nîmes, and a prehistoric shelter at Istres. In the Vaucluse, Beaumes-de-Venise has a paleochristian necropolis and probable prehistoric caves of Ambrosi on the hillside. Near Bollène is the neolithic troglodyte village of Barry, and the *bories* (stone shelters) at Bonnieux, known as the Claparedes, are said to be prehistoric. At Mallemort du Comtat the Unang caves have paleolithic deposits. At the foot of the Ventoux range, near Mormaison Loiron, paleolithic remains called l'Atelier des Sablons, have been found. Around Pertuis much evidence of the neolithic age has been found − silex, axes, pottery, Bronze Age arrowheads and tumuli mounds. Roaix, Ste Cecile-les-Vignes and caves at St Saturnin d'Apt have also been identified as neolithic villages.

Villes-sur-Auzon has many paleolithic, neolithic (and Gallo-Roman) remains. In the prehistory museum at Sault in the Vaucluse are many of the Mount Ventoux finds of weapons and coins. The Oppidum Celto-Ligure, Plateau d'Entremont, north of Aix is an excellent working site (visited by bus from Cours Sextius).

A brief history of Provence

The earliest tribesmen in this region known to historians were the Ligurians, around modern Aix were the Saluvii, around Avignon the Cavarii, near Apt the Vulgienti and elsewhere the Perreal and Cimbri. The tribe of Glanici, derived from the seventh-century god Glanis, lived at St Remy-de-Provence. A Celto-Ligurian burial place has been found at Roque Pertuse, west of Aix. The first colonisers were the Greeks from the Phocean islands of Ionia, who arrived by sea in the sixth-century BC and founded Massalia, modern Marseille. A Greek oppidum, called Castellan at Istres, can be seen near the Rhône entrance. Protis was their leader and they managed to co-exist with the north Africans from Carthage who arrived in 542 BC and remained for 60 years. The historian Posidonius recorded these facts in his second-century BC writings. The intrepid trader, Pytheas of Massalia, made several voyages around 340 BC to northern waters in search of tin which he found in Devon, and amber, for which he bartered wine with the natives. Immigrants also arrived from Rhodes, after whom the great River Rhône was named. So Marseille lays claim to being the oldest city in France – certainly it was a prosperous trading centre 2,500 years ago. It still has the remains of a Greek theatre, a Greek wall called Crinas and a Greek garden called des Vestiges.

About 271 BC, the Celto-Ligurians and Greek colonisers allied themselves with a Roman army to defeat the Carthaginians, although some 50 years later Hannibal marched through Spain, into Provence at Sisteron and across the Alps to invade northern Italy. His famous army of 70,000 men and equally famous 37 elephants were defeated and Provençal links with Rome increased. In 128 BC, Caius Sextius

31

Calvinius defeated a huge army of Celts, invaders from the north. His sixth legion founded Aquae Sextia Saluviorum, which became modern Aix-en-Provence. The medicinal spa waters and sub-tropical climate were much to the liking of the veteran legionnaires. Another Roman Consul, Caius Marius, saved Provence in 102 BC by defeating northern Teutons and Cimbrians at the foot of the Mountain of Ste Victoire. For the next five centuries the Pax Romana were most beneficial for their major province outside Italy, thus known as Provincia, and in 10 BC Emperor Augustus imposed direct rule. Aix, then Nîmes in the second century AD and Arles in the fourth century AD became the regional capitals. Marseille blotted their copybook because the inhabitants backed Pompey in the civil war against Julius Caesar, who promptly took very severe sanctions against them. Effectively their power and wealth was transferred to the three other cities and in 49 BC their maritime trade was neutralised. Nevertheless Pliny had commended the wines of Gigondas — so Aix was still in favour!

The decline and fall of the Roman Empire, c. 476 AD, affected most of Europe, and the rich Roman Provincia was a juicy morsel. The long dark nights came again. Invasions with sack and rapine arrived with unfailing and terrifying regularity: the Visigoths, Vandals, Alamans, Franks, the Saxons in 574 AD and Saracens in 726 AD — followed by the Moors and Saracens again in 838 AD, the Normans in the Camargue in 859 AD, and in Arles and Nîmes. Even the horrible Hungarians invaded in 924 AD. Looking back it seems incredible that anybody or any building survived the five centuries of savage incursion and looting, of death and desolation.

Medieval Provence

Provence was saved by incorporation into the Holy Roman Empire in 1032 AD and the Crusaders gathered at the southern ports, including Aigues-Mortes, to speed their fleets and armies in equally sacred aggression toward the Holy Land. Scattered through Provence are the holy relics 'looted' from Saladin's lands and distributed in a score of churches (St Anne's shroud in Apt, for instance). Knights Templars Commanderies and Priories can still be seen in many villages of the Vaucluse as they enjoyed their three centuries of fame and wealth before the French king proscribed their order.

The Counts of Provence and the warrior lords of Les Baux brought peace and some prosperity back to the region. Certainly the five Popes at Avignon in the fourteenth century encouraged every possible supplier to their papal courts including the growers of vinous Chateauneuf-du-Pape: painters, writers, musicians, sculptors, jewellers supplied the 82 Cardinals and their huge retinues with all they needed to maintain their luxurious way of life.

Good King René of Anjou was the most famous Count of Provence and undoubtedly the fifteenth century was the apogee of fame for Provence. He encouraged the arts, was a very popular *bon viveur* with the common touch and the Provencaux adored him. But on his death his nephew ceded Provence in 1481 to King Louis XI of France.

A quick summary of the Roman antiquities

Triumphal arches	At Orange (Marius Aurelius), Glanum (Augustus), Carpentras and Cavaillon
Mausoleums	At Glanum (Agrippa family), Arles, Alleins and St Julien-les-Martigues, Mazan and Alyscamps at Arles
Roman bridges	A superb example at Vaison; the Pont Julien (River Coulon west of Apt); and the Pont Flavian (River Touloubre SE of St Chamas)
Aqueducts	The Pont de Gard is world famous: lesser examples are to be seen at Meyrargues, SE of Pertuis; Barbegal aqueducts SE of Fontvielle

Town gates	Augustus gate at Cavaillon; Nîmes; Arles
Theatre	Orange (quite superb), Arles, Vaison-la-Romaine and Apt (with much imagination)
Thermal baths	Aix; Apt; Mont Cavalier in Nîmes
Temples	Part of Aix Cathedral; Nîmes (to Diana); Fontvielle/Glanum (to Cybele) and Maison Carré at Nîmes (the most elegant)
Amphitheatres	Nîmes; Arles (both designed by Titus Crispius Reburrus)
Villas	Glanum and Vaison-la-Romaine
Fountains and gardens	Nîmes (Jardin de la Fontaine)
Watchtowers	Tour Magne in Nîmes (possible victory memorial)
Gymnasium	Orange near the Theatre
Museums (with Roman finds)	Nîmes (Museum of Antiquities); Arles (Pagan Art); Aix (Beaux Arts) and Vaison-la-Romaine
Water distribution	The Castellum basin in Nîmes
Canals	Marius canal built 104 BC through the swamps from Arles to Fos on the coast
Roads	The Via Agrippa is now the modern RN7; the Via Aurelia went from Rome to the Rhône Valley thence north to Britain. The Via Domitia led from NE Spain via Provence to Rome

As a matter of historical fact the Provencaux have always been a 'difficult' tribe. They supported the Albigensiens in the twelfth to thirteenth centuries before Simon de Montfort was ordered (and paid) by the French King to exterminate them. The local protesting sect of Vaudois were eventually massacred in 1545 by the army of King Francis I. The Huguenots of the sixteenth century were the majority creed in many Provençal towns including Nîmes, although Marseille remained Catholic. At the massacre of St Bartholomew in 1572 thousands of Huguenots were murdered, imprisoned (for instance in Aigues-Mortes) or condemned to the galleys of Toulon and Marseille. This persecution continued, and even accelerated at the end of the seventeenth century under Louis XIV. At the beginning of the eighteenth century two curious historical contradictions occurred. The Principality of Orange Nassau (modern Netherlands) ruled the town and region of Orange in Provence. For a brief moment in 1713 the Dutch King and Queen (William and Mary of Orange) became the English royal family and thus controlled part of Provence! Conversely the Jacobite Pretenders were given sanctuary in Provence, particularly at Aix. Gentlemen from England, with their ladies on the Grand Tour, often reported in their diaries of meetings with their Jacobite counterparts in Provence.

Like most of Europe, this region, with its great ports, was always vulnerable to ship-borne diseases. Outbreaks of plague or Black Death occurred in 1339, 1348, 1361 and again in 1580, and finally in 1720 when 100,000 of the population of Provence lost their lives.

The French Revolution

Towards the end of the eighteenth century the start of the French Revolution brought chaos. The competent bourgeois (mayors, lawyers, priests and all local dignatories) were arraigned, humiliated and usually guillotined. Most of the handsome abbeys and châteaux were destroyed.

Marseille was a real revolutionary city in the spring of 1789 and Rouget de Lisle's song *Le Chant des Marseillais* was to become famous. In neighbouring Martigues the tricoleur flag originated (blue for Ferrières, red for Jonquières and white for the Ile). In 1792 five hundred volunteers from Marseille marched to Paris singing the 'Marseillaise'; the guillotine on the Canebière was kept as busy with the falling heads of the aristos and bourgoisie as in Paris. In the name, of course, of 'Liberté, Egalité et Fraternité', lovely abbeys and churches were destroyed. Predictably enough, Provence failed to support Napoleon when he made himself Emperor of the French and the 'white terror' claimed many victims in the region.

From the eighteenth century onwards

The Age of the Grand Tour in the eighteenth and nineteenth centuries brought hundreds of young English milords and their tutors to see the Roman antiquities in Arles, Orange and Avignon on their way to Rome and Florence.

The prosperous mid-nineteenth century saw the foundation of the Provençal literary group, the Félibrige (1854) led by Frédéric Mistral who published his poem 'Mireio' (1859). This great Provençal poet (1830-1914) had a profound influence and his museums in Maillane and Arles (the Arlaten) should be visited. In the mid-nineteenth century the new railways linked Marseille, Avignon and Nîmes with Paris. Mark Twain and other American visitors certainly appreciated this new form of travel.

The phylloxera plague of 1880 destroyed many vineyards in Provence and fruit orchards were planted as replacement crops. The First World War, from 1914–18, decimated the region of its young men who died in Flanders, and the Second World War brought occupation from 1942-4 by the Germans. Local resistance groups were formed and helped the Allied landings in August 1944. Many towns, however, were severely damaged by the American Air Force bombardments or by the Wehrmacht (Marseille 1943). The last fifty years have seen Provence become more prosperous than ever before. Tourism, the huge oil complexes around Marseille, the influx of *pieds noirs* from Algeria (1962), the new A6 and A7 motorways that link Paris and Marseille and the dynamics of the French provincial towns and cities have all contributed to this success.

For the record, the main cities in Provence with their present population are:

Marseille	880,000
Nîmes	130,000
Aix-en-Provence	125,000
Avignon	91,000
Arles	51,000
Salon-de-Provence	36,000
Orange	27,500
Carpentras	26,000

Old Provençal folklore and customs can be seen and studied in the following museums:

Arles	Musée Arlaten, closed Monday - the best
Aix	Musée du Vieil Aix, closed Monday and February
Carpentras	Musée Comtadin, closed Wednesday
Marseille	Musée du Vieux Marseille, closed Tuesday, Wednesday a.m.
Nîmes	Musée de Vieux Nîmes, closed Sunday a.m. and Tuesdays in winter
Avignon	Theodore Aubanel Museum, closed weekends
Maillane	Frédéric Mistral Museum, closed Monday
St Remy de Provence	Musée des Alpilles, Pl. de Brun, closed Tuesday
Les Stes-Maries	Musée Baroncelli, closed Wednesday
	Boumian Museum, open April – end October

37

Château-Gombert	Museum of Art and Traditions, closed Tuesday
Camargue	Musée Camarguais, Pont de Rousty, closed winter, Tuesday
Orange	Musée Comtadin

Citizens of Provence

Theodore Aubanel (1829-86)	Co-founder of Provence, Félibrige society (museum in Avignon)
Folco de Baroncelli,	19th-century patron of Camargue
Marquess Baux, lords of (10-14th centuries)	Warrior barons of Les Baux
Jacques Bernus (1650-1728)	Church sculptor from Mazan
Henri Bosco	20th-century novelist/poet from Lourmarin
Yves Brayer	20th-century painter (see Réattu Museum
Esprit Calvet	19th-century Avignon doctor, donated library (see museum)
Blaise Cendrars	Marseille writer of 19th century
Jules Cantini	Marseille sculptor of 19th century
Paul Cézanne (1839–1906)	Aix's most famous painter
Enguerrand Charonton (Quartron)	15th-century Provençal painter
Jean Chapuis	18th-century painter of Avignon
Jean Chastel, (1726–93)	Aix sculptor (fountains etc)
Le Corbusier (1887–1965)	Marseille architect of La Cité Radieuse
Adam de Craponne (1527–76)	Civil engineer of Salon de Provence
Alphonse Daudet (1840–97)	Writer Lettres de Mon Moulin, Tartarin de Tarascon
Duplessis (1725–1802)	Painter of Carpentras (see museum)

Frédérique Duran	20th-century painter, glassmaker (museum near Gordes)
Esperandieu (1829-74)	Architect of Marseille Cathedral
Jean Henri Fabre (1823–1915)	Natural history writer from Serignan
Nicholas Froment (15th century)	Famous early Avignon painter to King René
François Marius Granet	19th-century Aix painter, friend of Ingres
Louis Grobet	19th-century Marseille musician (see museum)
Paul Guigou	19th-century landscape painter from Aix
Inguimbertine	Bishop of Carpentras, donated library 1745
Josse Lieferinxe	15th-century Provençal painter of Avignon
Jean Lurcat	19th-century Arles tapestry maker (museum)
Jean Louis Laquel	17th-century Santon-maker of Aubagne
Charles Maurras	19th-century writer of Martigues
Gabriel Mirabeau, Count (1749–91)	French revolutionary leader of Aix
Frédéric Mistral (1830–1914)	Great Provençal poet, Nobel prizewinner
Mignards	Famous 19th-century Provençal family of painters (Nicholas)
François Mansard	19th-century Marseille architect
Michel de Nostradamus (1503–66)	Physician, prophet, astrologer from Salon de Provence
Marcel Pagnol (1895–1974)	20th-century Marseille writer, film maker
Abbé Papon	18th-century Provençal historian
Parrocels	Famous 19th-century family of painters
Pierre Puget (1620–94)	Marseille artist, architect – famous talented family

Francisco Petrarch (1304–74)	Italian poet resident in Provence
Pradier	19th-century sculptor from Nîmes
Jacques Réattu (1760–1833)	Painter from Arles (see museum)
Joseph Roumanille (19th century)	Co-founder of Félibrige society
René of Anjou, Count of Provence (1409–80)	Most favoured ruler
Sades, family	Notable family of St Rémy including husband of Laura
Marie de Sevigné, Madame	17th-century writer, lived at Château de Grignan
Van Loo family (18th century)	Dutch family of painters, worked in Aix
Joseph Vernet	18th-century painter from Avignon
Louis Vouland	19th-century Avignon doctor, donated library
Felix Ziem (1821–1911)	19th-century painter from Martigues (see museum)
Emile Zola (1840–1902)	Famous writer, born and brought up in Aix

CHAPTER FOUR:
LAND OF SAINTS AND LEGENDS

More than any other area of France, Provence had the closest
links with the Holy Land, and the Holy Family. About thirteen
years after the Crucifixion, a boat without oars or sails landed
on the shores of what has been known since as Les Stes
Maries-de-la-Mer, to the west side of the Camargue triangle.
On board were the Virgin Mother's sister St Mary Jacobe, the
mother of the Apostles James and John, St Mary Salome,
and St Mary Magdalene (i.e. the three Saintes Maries).
Accompanying them were four other saints: Martha, Lazarus,
Maximin and the blind Suedonius (Lazarus was the brother to
Mary Magdalene and Martha). Finally came black Sarah, their
African servant. Soon the evangelists split up, leaving the
Maries and Sarah in the small community where an oratory
was built. They were eventually buried in the massive church,
Sarah in the fifteenth-century crypt and the two Maries in the
chapel above the apse. Now it is a place of frequent
pilgrimage, particularly by the Romanies and Gitanes of
Europe who adopted Sarah as their patron saint. Eventually
the little band of saints decided to spread the gospel inland.

Martha then went to Tarascon, where she tamed a fabulous
Rhône monster with holy water and the sign of the cross.
Lazarus, with his sisters and St Maximin, lived for some time
in a catacomb in the cemetery of St Victor in Marseille. St
Maximin and Suedonius then went to Aix, where the former
became its first bishop and was martyred for his faith. The
tombs in the crypt of the Basilique of St Maximin-la-Sainte-
Bonne, 40 km east of Aix, have been venerated as being that
of St Mary Magdalene and of St Maximin.

The four sarcophagi in the oratory are amongst the oldest
Christian relics in France. Legend has it that the Jews of

Jerusalem cast adrift the boat with the Holy Family in it.
Ironically enough, Provence has been a sanctuary for Jewish
communities, and synagogues have been well established in
Carpentras, Avignon, Cavaillon and L'Isle-sur-la-Sorgue.

Religious legends

Mary Magdalen spent her last 33 years of life in a cave known
as Ste Baume (*Baume* is Provençal for cave), east of
Gemenos. Just before her death she came to meet, and
receive Communion from, St Maximin, close to where the
abbey of that name now stands.

According to legend, Christ appeared in person in Arles to
the Greek apostle St Trophimus, who had been sent there by
St Peter to help evangelise Provence. And St Remigius, *c.*
500 AD, exorcised a young girl at Glanum (St Rémy-de-
Provence) — she died, but he brought her back to life and
was duly canonised.

Christian communities sprang up all over Provence in the
third century. There were Christian Bishops of Arles and
Emperor Constantine recognised Christianity in the fourth
century, which competed with the cults of the sun god Mithras
and goddess Cybele. Poor St Victor was martyred in the third
century at Marseille on the present site of the Basilica. It was
at Arles that Constantine held the first council of Christian
bishops in 314 AD. A curious link with Britain occurred in
Arles in 597 AD when St Virgil, Bishop of Arles, consecrated
St Augustin, the first Bishop of England.

Another legend says that Balthazar — one of the three
original Magi, or Wise Men, appearing at the Nativity — went
to live at Les Baux-de-Provence. He, it was said, was the
founder member of that extraordinary warlike tribe who
dominated much of southern France (and Albania!) from their
eagle's eyrie. Of course, Provence was Crusader country. Not
only did the Knights Templars build and fortify a score or
more of Commanderies but their comrades brought back
many relics of the saints as trophies from the Holy Land. St
Anne in the basilica at Apt is just one example.

Yet another legend has it that in 1177 Christ spoke to
Benezet, as a shepherd boy aged 12, and instructed him to

build the bridge of 22 arches across the River Rhône at Avignon.

The Abbey of St Ruf, built in the ninth century, commemorates St Ruf, the son of Simon of Cyrene, who once helped Christ carry his cross.

In Apt, the Cathedral of St Anne contains 'St Anne's shroud'. She was the mother of the Virgin Mary and legend has it that her body was brought to France and lies buried here. On the last Sunday in July a major pilgrimage is held to see the shrine, the shroud and reliquary bust of the saint.

St Genesius, the patron saint of Arles, a clerk and writer, was martyred by the Romans when he refused to take down a decree banning the Christian faith.

The tomb of St Romanus is to be found in the abbey of that name near Beaucaire, opposite Tarascon, and that of St Giles the Hermit who gave his money to the poor in the eighth century and is buried in the church of that name west of Arles.

One of the most attractive legends is of St Pilon on the crossroads of the Col du St Pilon (near Ste Baume). There angels bore Mary Magdalene seven times a day so that she could hear the music of Paradise.

Another legend is that Charlemagne's heroes of the battle of Roncevaux are buried in the Alyscamps cemetery at Arles (possible but unlikely).

Sanctuaries of respite

Several villages in Provence — usually in the Vaucluse — have cemeteries *only* for small children, often carved out of a rockface. The tradition is that if the infant died before it had been baptised, and the parents brought the seemingly dead babe to this 'sanctuary of respite', life would be miraculously but briefly restored. There would be sufficient time for a baptismal mass to be said before final burial. One such village is at St Pantaleon, east of Cavaillon on the D60.

Pilgrimages

Provence has a number of annual pilgrimages and two of the most important take place each year at Les Stes Maries-de-la-Mer. On the 24/25 May gitanes, nomads and travellers from all over Europe — the Romany family — gather to pay their respects to dusky Sarah, the saint of the gypsies. Young couples get married, infants are baptised and masses are said in the old fortified church — a refuge from the Saracen invaders. The bones of the three saints, Mary Jacobe, Mary Salome and their maidservant, black Sarah, were discovered in 1448 and King René ordered a crypt to be built to contain the reliquaries. The two-day pilgrimage has been kept ever since. On the Sunday nearest to 22 October another takes place, with a procession and blessing of the sea from whence the saints arrived in a little blue boat!

Other pilgrimages take place at Notre-Dames-de-Lumières on the D60 east of Cavaillon, where there is a seventeenth-century black virgin. In 1661 mysterious lights were seen by a mortally sick farmer who subsequently survived! Others take place at St Michel-de-Frigolet Abbey, at Graveson (a pilgrimage to St Anthime on 27 April), at Roque-sur-Pernes (on 15 May to St Gens who used to tame lions and persuade the heavens to loose rain) and at Monteaux-le-Beaucet (St Gens again on 15 May and St John's in September). There are many more minor pilgrimages about which the local tourist office will advise.

Legendary animals

The most famous of the early medieval animals is the Tarasque, tamed by St Martha at Tarascon. It was said to be part crocodile, part lion and part amphibious dragon! To the east of Brignoles in the Var is Draguignan, where mystical local dragons gave their name to the town. Similarly, Couleuvre was the source of mystical serpents. Tauroentum is or was the ancient submerged city off Pointe Connière (west of Marseille), where at dead of night a massive bull comes ashore to feed off the local grapes. A fabulous golden goat — the *chevre d'or* — is or was to be found north near Valréas, and at Glanum and Les Baux.

Provence — land of legends.

CHAPTER FIVE:
WHO WROTE WHAT ABOUT PROVENCE

For two thousand years writers and poets have been extolling the charms and beauty of this region. First of all there were the Greeks and the Romans, the troubadours (although they were pursuing more immediate and tangible rewards), and the Italian poet Petrarch in the fourteenth century (although he had Laura more on his mind than anything else). French writers such as Madame de Sevigné, Alphonse Daudet, Stendahl, Mistral, Prosper Merimée and Camus, have left us their views on the people and the countryside. Anglo-Saxon writers too have recorded their sympathies for Provence – such as our nineteenth-century professional travellers the Scots novelist Tobias Smollett, English agronomist Arthur Young, Charles Dickens, Wordsworth, and more recently Lawrence Durrell and Gertrude Stein. Mark Twain fell in love with Marseille and his *A Tramp Abroad* or *Innocents Abroad* make delightful reading.

I have chosen a short collection which only skims the surface of the dedicated Provence-lover's anthology.

Greek and Roman writers

One of the earliest comments came from the Greek Posidonius writing in the second century BC. 'The country is wild and arid . . . work is an ungrateful toil.' Even today, much of Provence soil is poor and barren, particularly in parts of the Camargue and the hinterland mountain slopes. Fortunately lavender seems to thrive on poor soil and many vines and olive trees will grow and flourish in stony ground.

The Roman Emperor Honorius wrote in 418 AD, 'Arles is so fortunately placed, its commerce is so active and merchants come in such numbers that all the products of the universe are channelled there; the riches of the Orient, perfumes of Arabia, delicacies of Assyria.'

Some later impressions of Provence

It must be admitted that the dozens of troubadours who lived in Provence, such as Raoult de Gassin and Raimbaud of Orange, spent little time describing or praising their countryside. Epic and passionate poems of gallantry, love and amorous indiscretions were their forte in the twelfth and thirteenth centuries. Petrarch too in the fourteenth century 'beheld a sweet young damsel of Provence', but his 366 poems of the Canzonière were mostly devoted to Laura's charms. He was scathing, however, about Avignon's dissipation − 'a sink of iniquity', he called it.

Towards the end of the seventeenth century, Madame de Sevigné was living in Grignan and writing to her daughter of her visits to the country. A bon viveur, she described the Provençal cuisine with gusto − the succulent doves, the tender quail, the partridges fed on Provençal herbs to give them extra flavour, the muscat grapes, figs and melons were quite perfect. But, like all observers of the scene, she feared the Rhône valley mistral wind, 'bitter and freezing which cuts one's being to the quick'. She described Apt as a 'a jam cauldron'.

Tobias Smollett, a Scots novelist who lived for a time in Provence in 1763, wrote 'If I lived at Nismes or Avignon I should take pleasure in forming parties to come hither in summer to dine under one of the arches of the Pont-du-Gard on a cold collation'. He travelled by mule-carriage and described the Roman viaduct (six arches, then a tier of eleven lower arches, and on the top no less than thirty-five even smaller arches carrying in a covered channel, five feet deep, water from Uzès to Nimes) as. 'A piece of architecture so unaffectedly elegant, so simple and majestic that I will defy the most phlegmatic and stupid spectator to behold it without admiration.' All the young milords on the Grand Tour *had* to visit the Pont-du-Gard as part of their 'education'. But Smollett also wrote 'this asthmatic and blustering country', but then he might have been describing himself.

John Keats (1795−1821) quoted Provence on several occasions in the 'Eve of St Agnes': 'He play'd an ancient ditty, long since mute, in Provence call'd "la belle dame sans mercy" '.

In 'Ode to a Nightingale', he wrote 'O for a draught of vintage! that hath been/ Cool'd a long age in the deep-delved earth/ Tasting of Flora and the Country-green/ Dance and Provençal song, and sunburnt mirth.'

Elizabeth Barret Browning (1806–61) wrote, 'Even now I walk as in a dream. We made a pilgrimage from Avignon to Vaucluse in right poetical duty; the scenery is full of grandeur, the rooks sheathe themselves into the sky.'

William Wordsworth (1770-1850) wrote,

'The day at Vaucluse where I was enchanted with the power and beauty of the stream and the wildness and grandeur of the rocks – much pleased with Nismes, with Marseille, but most of all with the drive between Marseille and Toulon, singularly romantic and varied. One of the few promises of summer which we have had is the peach blossom abundantly scattered over some parts of the country and very beautiful when neighboured by the cypress.'

But the little Corsican (Napoleon Bonaparte) took a more jaundiced view of the people after an attempt had been made on his life when on his way to Elba. *'C'est une méchante race que les Provençaux.'* (These Provençaux are a wicked lot.)

Prosper Merimée, Inspecteur Général des Monuments de France, published a book in 1835 *Notes d'un Voyage dans le Midi de la France*. He commented on the rose trees and olive trees on the banks of the Rhône, on the Andalusian atmosphere of Avignon, the thick patois of the natives. Of the Pont-du-Gard he wrote 'Le site sauvage, la solitude complete du lieu, le bruit du torrent, ajoutaient une poesie sublime à l'architecture imposante qui s'offrant à mes yeux.'

Charles Dickens (1812–70) wrote 'There lay before us that same afternoon the broken bridge of Avignon and all the city baking in the sun: yet with an under-done-pie-crust, battlemented wall that never will be brown, tho' it bake for centuries.'

Henry James' book of 1881, *A Little Tour of France*, was in fact a Grand Tour of Provence.

'It was a pleasure to feel oneself in Provence again – the land where the silver grey earth is impregnated with the light of the sky . . . I became more intimate with that Provençal charm which I had already enjoyed from the window of the train and which glowed in the sweet sunshine and the white rocks and lurked in the smoke puffs of the little olives. The olive trees in Provence are half the landscape . . . this mild colourless bloom seems the very texture of the country.'

He wrote chapters about Nîmes and the Pont du Gard, Aigues-Mortes, Les Baux, Tarascon and Avignon and fell in love with Marseille.

Of Avignon, young Mrs Anna Jameson, the art historian, wrote in the mid-nineteenth century, 'We are in the *south* here, olive trees, figs, vines at every step,' even though their voyage by boat from Lyons southwards had been in incessant rain, and a hot crowded cabin on board their 'dirty steamboat'.

Alphonse Daudet wrote his *Lettres de Mon Moulin* in 1868 partly in Paris, partly in the château d'Amboy, and possibly in or near the celebrated windmill outside Fontvieille. Translated, he noted 'At other times we would arrange to meet at the town of Les Baux, that dusty pile of ruins, sharp rocks and old emblazoned palaces, crumbling, quivering in the wind like high eagles' nests!' His comic non-hero Tartarin of Tarascon has helped put that Provençal town on the map, however slighting his references were at the time!

The American writer Henry James, visiting Arles in 1870 and 1882, in his *A Little Tour of France* wrote of the Musée Lapidaire in the Sainte Anne Church 'the most Roman thing I know of out of Rome', and of the Roman theatre at Arles 'one of the most charming and touching ruins that I had ever beheld . . . one of the sweetest legacies of the ancient world.'

I wish I had more space to quote more of Henry James, but one final piece will suffice.

'We knew in advance that Les Baux was a pearl of picturesqueness. The drive itself was charming for there is an inexhaustible sweetness in the grey-green landscape of Provence. It blooms with heath and scented shrubs and

stunted olive and the white rock shining through the
scattered herbage has a brightness which answers to the
brightness of the sky. Listen to the hum of bees and the
whistle of melancholy shepherds. Nothing can be prettier
than the crags of Provence: they are beautifully modelled
as painters say and they have a delightful silvery colour.'

When James had climbed the hill and explored Les Baux he
called it a 'medieval Pompeii'.

Modern writings

More recently Hilaire Belloc wrote lovingly of Provence 'where
the public monuments of antiquity bear witness more than in
any other place to the Roman foundations of Europe.' And
Lawrence Durrell in his novel *Monsieur* writes of 'Avignon,
honey-coloured, rose faded walls and machicolated towers
rising steeply from a country dusted silver with olive.'

Vladimir Nabokov writes 'Provence . . . I wander aimlessly
from lane to lane bending a careful ear to ancient times –
the same cicadas sang in Caesar's reign upon the wall, the
same sun clings and climbs . . .'

James Pope-Hennessy's *Aspects of Provence*, of 1952,
emphasised the beauty of the Provençal skies.

'On the plain of Maillane and St Rémy the sky can
sometimes seem more important than the earth for here
above the low green land the dawns and sunsets quiver
– magenta changing to pale apple-green; scarlet to deep
yellow – and at mid-day the sky is as blue as in the
tropics.'

Rudyard Kipling, Katherine Mansfield, Stendhal, and
Gertrude Stein who lived in 1922 at St Rémy, have all contributed to the literature of Provence. But the indisputable
local 'patriot' was Frédéric Mistral who, in 1854, founded a
society of local poets near Avignon called the Félibrige.
Aubanel, the local printer, and Joseph Roumanille, the local
schoolmaster, were among the original seven founder
members. The object of the society was to keep the genuine

Provençal language and folklore alive and not let it be swamped by modern civilisation. (He could not forsee the huge oil complex and harbour networks of Marseille and Fos.) Mistral's romantic 'Mireio' was set to music by Gounod and his *Tresor du Félibrige* (1879–86), which is *the* dictionary of Provençal phrases and language, was his masterpiece (and can be read in the British Library). No wonder that in 1905 Mistral was awarded the Nobel prize for literature, and that enabled him to endow and found the marvellous Museum Arlaten in Arles (to which every lover of Provence should pay a visit).

Another museum, Museum Mistral, can be visited in his small home village of Maillane, NE of Tarascon. It is fitting, therefore, to include his brief poem 'Mireio'.

MIREIO

O magnefiqui souloumbrado!
De frais, d'aubo desmesurado
Miraiavon, di bord, si pège blanquinous;
De lambrusco antico, bestorto,
l'envertouiavon si redorto,
E dóu cimèu di branco forto
Leissavon pendoula si pampagnoun sinous.

Lou Rose, emé sis oundo lasso,
E dourmihouso, e tranquilasso,
Passavo; e regretous dóu palais d'Avignoun,
Di farandoulo e di sinfòni,
Coumo un grand vièi qu'es a l'angòni,
Eu pareissié tout malancòni
D'ana perdre à la mar e sis aigo e soun noum.

Frédéric Mistral completed this unique epic poem in 1858 and dedicated it to Lamartine. He wrote in the rich and colourful Provençal language and set the tragic love-story of Mireille and Vincent against the thyme-scented landscapes of the southern Rhône. In these verses, he sings of this mighty river, 'Lou Rose'.

CHAPTER SIX:
THE PAINTERS OF PROVENCE

The stark brilliant harsh light swept clean by the mistral wind has inspired painters over the centuries to depict the Provençal scene: the landscapes of course, mountains, valleys and rivers, cypress and olive trees, poppy fields and the Roman antiquities, as well as the everyday village life of cafés, landladies and canal-bridges.

The Avignon papacy in the fourteenth century − seven French Popes and scores of rich cardinals, each with their appropriate palace − encouraged artists from all over Europe to come to Provence. Clement V was the first serious patron of the arts. Some of the best Flemish and Italian painters arrived to paint triptyches, frescoes, religious scenes and occasional portraits. Simone Martini (1285-1344) of Siena, who worked for the French kings in Naples, was the first painter of significance. His frescoes can be seen in the Palais des Papes (originally in Notre-Dame-des-Doms Cathedral).

Fifteenth-century artists

Enguerrand Charonton, Quartron, or Chartron, was born in Caen in 1416 and became a master painter in Avignon by 1444. He also painted in Arles and Aix. One of his masterpieces, painted in 1453, the *Coronation of the Virgin*, is in the Hospice des Villeneuve-lès-Avignon. His *Virgin of Mercy* is in the Musée Condé at Chantilly, and his *Virgin and Child between Two Saints* is in the Musée du Petit Palais in Avignon. He was regarded as the master painter of the primitive Avignon School.

King René of Anjou was a great patron of the arts. He

sponsored not only Charonton but also Nicholas Froment (1436-86) and Jean Chapuis. The former's greatest work is the *Burning Bush*, symbolising the virginity of Mary, but also tactfully showing his patron and second wife kneeling in prayer, which can be seen in the Cathedral of St Sauveur at Aix-en-Provence. Froment was born in Uzès near Nîmes and in addition to his triptych and his *Martyrdom of St Mitre* being in Aix, the Uffizi in Florence has his *Resurrection of Lazarus*, painted in 1461.

Jean Chapuis, or Chapus, painted a lovely *Virgin's Annunciation* which can be seen in the Church of Ste Marie Madeleine in Aix. To see the best collection of these fifteenth century primitives, visit the Musée Calvet in Avignon.

King René also commissioned works from Francesco Laurana (1488), whose *Bearing of the Cross* is to be seen in the church of St Didier in Avignon, and from Barthelemy de Clive.

It was not until the seventeenth century that a resurgence of art took place again. Perhaps the terrible wars of religion in the sixteenth century inhibited creativity and rich patrons were few and far between.

Notable painting families

The large Parrocel family lived in Avignon and produced many very competent painters. Louis, who was born in 1640, produced historical paintings. Pierre, born in 1664, studied in Rome and Paris and his *Coronation of the Virgin* is to be seen in St Mary's church in Marseille. Pierre Ignace Parrocel, born in 1702, studied in Rome 1739–40 and etched 36 plates of Bernini's statues. A grandson, Charles Parrocel, later painted King Louis XIV. Another Avignon family of painters were the Mignards, a father and son called Nicholas. After studying in Rome, the son painted biblical works and became court painter to Louis XIV. His son Paul also painted in Avignon.

Altarpieces painted by Parrocels and Mignards can be seen in the churches of St Pierre, St Agricol and St Symphorien in Avignon, in Carpentras in the Duplessis Museum and chapel in the Hôtel Dieu, and in the Musée Réattu in Arles.

The Daret family, Jean and his sons Michel and Jean Baptiste, came from Brussels to Aix early in the seventeenth century. Jean (1613–68) painted *Portrait of a Magistrate,* now in the Fine Arts Museum of Marseille.

Another remarkable painting family were the Van Loos. Jacob, born in 1614, was a Flemish painter. His son, Jean Baptiste (1684–1745), was born in Aix and became a notable portrait painter. He married Marguerite Le Brun in Toulon, sister of the Parisian painter. He then worked in Nice, Monaco, Genoa, Turin and Rome. In 1737 he went to London and Sir Robert Walpole became his patron. Van Loo painted the Prince and Princess of Wales, Colley Cibber and Owen MacSwinney. He returned to Aix and lived in the Pavillon de Vendôme where he died in 1745. His works can be seen in the Louvre, Brussels, Darmstadt, London and in Provençal museums and churches. His son Carlo Van Loo (1705–65) was born in Nice and his *St Francis* is in the church of Ste Marthe in Tarascon. François Van Loo was born in Aix but died studying in Turin. Louis Michel Van Loo (1707–71) was born in Toulon, studied in Rome and Paris and became Court painter to Philip V of Spain. The Musée Cheret in Nice has a good collection of highly coloured Van Loos.

Seventeenth–century artists

Perhaps the most famous – certainly the most talented – artist of the seventeenth century was Pierre Puget, born in 1622 in Marseille. He studied in Rome, Florence, Aix, Toulon and Genoa. When he became ill in 1655 he gave up painting and took to sculpture and architecture! By the time he died in 1694 he had become one of the greatest sculptors in France. Some of his major works are in the Musée des Beaux Arts in Marseille (*The Faun, The Plague at Milan* and *Louis XIV riding)*; in Toulon Town Hall; in the Granet Museum in Aix (self-portrait) and the Musée Arbaud (portrait of his mother). His sons Pierre and François followed in his footsteps.

A turn of the century sculptor-painter was Jacques Bernus de Mazan (1650–1728), whose works can be seen in Carpentras, the museum in Mazan 5 km away and Montbrun-les-Bains. Other sculptors of note were Jean Antoine Houdin

(1741–1828) in the Granet Museum and Jean Chastel (1726–1793) of Aix (Post Office/Cornmarket).

Eighteenth-century artists

Carpentras – a town not noted for its tradition of painting – houses the Musée Duplessis. Joseph Duplessis (1725–1802) was taught to paint by his father and studied in Rome, Lyon and Paris. His portraits of Gluck, Franklin and Abbé Bossuet are on show.

However, the most famous eighteenth-century masters were the Vernet family of Avignon. Antoine (1690–1753) fathered 22 children, of whom four became painters. Antoine Ignace (1726–75) studied at Naples and painted marine subjects. François Gabriel (1728–80) painted in the palaces of Fontainebleau and Versailles, and his flower studies can been seen in the Calvet Museum. Antoine Francois (1730–79) painted religious subjects. However, the eldest son, Claude Joseph Vernet (1714–89), was the most famous. From Avignon he went to Aix, then to Rome where he studied under Panini and adopted the style of Salvador Rosa. Then he went back to Paris where he died. His paintings are in the Louvre, National Gallery and the Calvet in Avignon, *L'Entrée du Port de Marseille* being one of his best-known works.

Hubert Robert (1733–1808) of Avignon studied in Italy with Fragonard, and his landscapes and ruins depict this influence. Many of his works are in the Louvre and the Calvet in Avignon. His best-known work is the *Pont-du-Gard.*

Pierre Raspay (1748–1825), also of Avignon, studied in Paris under Vernet. The Calvet has his *View of the Pope's Palace, View of the Bridge of St Benezet* and a portrait of *Abbé Juenet.*

François Marius Granet (1775–1849), a friend of Ingres, was a painter of historical and architectural scenes who studied under David in Paris. He donated five hundred works to found the museum bearing his name in Aix.

In the late eighteenth century Jacques Réattu (1760–1833) lived in Arles, studied in Paris under Regnault, won the Grande Prix of 1791, and decorated the theatre at Marseille.

He adopted the style of Corot. His daughters bought the Priory of the Knights of Malta in Arles which now houses the Musée Réattu. Réattu's uncle, Antoine Raspail, another painter, also has his works on show. Réattu's *History of St Paul* is in the Beauvais Museum.

The Impressionists

Despite this convincing background of artistic talent spread over six centuries, Provence is most famous for its Impressionist school. Paul Cézanne (1839–1906), and later Vincent Van Gogh (1853–90), found inspiration from the cypress and olives, the golden cornfields, ochre–coloured villages and the forbidding mountains of Ventoux. Paul Gauguin (1848–1903) visited Provence briefly in 1888 and shared a house with the unbalanced Dutchman, then living in Arles. Van Gogh wrote 'the pale orange of the sunsets make the fields appear blue'.

Henri Matisse (1869–1954), Maurice Vlaminck (1876–1958) and Raoul Dufy were deeply attracted to Cassis (SE of Marseille) and the three of them painted the blue sea, sky and orange–red cliffs. Vlaminck also painted in Arles and Jean Baptist Corot worked in Martigues. Some of the minor Impressionists were local Provençaux artists. Frédéric Bazille (1841–70) from Montpelier, a friend of Sisley, Monet and Renoir, painted one of my favourites – Aigues-Mortes in golden red and orange. Paul Guigoun (1834–71), whose works can be seen in the Musée des Beaux Arts in Marseille, also painted the Alyscamps cemetery at Arles and *Washerwomen on the banks of the River Durance*. Charles Camoin, born 1879, was a friend of Cézanne and painted in Provence. Felix Ziem (1821–1910) of Martigues, west of Marseille, painted the little fishing village as *Little Venice*.

But back to the two great masters. Paul Cézanne was born in Aix and was a lifelong friend of Emile Zola, with whom he went to school. By 1861 he was part of the painters' circle of the Café Guerbois, with Pissaro and Manet. For many years he failed to make any sales until a customs officer (the strangest of patrons), one Victor Choquet, purchased 35 canvases. By 1877 at the Impressionists' Exhibition in Paris, Cézanne's 16 paintings were the main attraction. When

Renoir and Monet visited Provence, Cézanne was resident in Aix at No. 23 Rue Boulegon. He was basing his style on sixteenth-century Venetian masters, but also on Poussin and Rubens. His atelier, appropriately sited at No. 9 Ave. Paul Cézanne, is near the Hospital of St Jaques in the northern quarter of Aix. The first floor was his study and it looks now exactly as it did on the day of his death in 1906. He painted the Mountain of Sainte Victoire many times, the L'Estaque hills and the Route de Tholonet (now called the Route Cézanne). Besides landscapes and still life paintings he will be remembered for his *Lake at Annecy*, a series of *Bathers*, the *Cardplayers, Bay of Marseille* and *Madame Cézanne in the greenhouse*.

Cézanne was also influenced by the style of another local Provençal painter, Honoré Daumier (1808–79). He was a talented man, born in Marseille, a painter and sculptor who also wrote political sketches and satires. This local school included Emile Loubon (1809–63), born in Aix, who became head of the school of drawing in Marseille. One of his best pictures is *Mineurs du tunnel de la Nerthe'*. Adolphe Monticelli (1842–86), was a protégé of Loubon, whose impasto technique influenced Van Gogh, Fleury, Richard and Paul Guigoun. In the Musée des Beaux Arts in Marseille can be seen many works by Monticelli, Richard, Guigoun and a ladypainter, Françoise Duparc, who worked much of her life in England.

Vincent Van Gogh (1853–90), born in Brabant, spent the last two years of his life in Arles and St Rémy — partly sane, partly insane. All the world knows how he cut off his right ear and then painted a self-portrait of his bandaged face and head! In Arles he found many subjects to his taste: the Café du Soir, Café du Nuit, the Yellow House, the Alyscamps, the drawbridge of Langlois, cornfields at sunset and, of course, the beautiful sunflowers. He spent a week at Stes Maries-de-la-Mer and there painted *A view of La Crau* and *Fishing boats on the beach at Stes Maries*. His energy was incredible. In 15 months he painted 300 canvases! In his life he painted a total of 600 paintings and 800 watercolours and drawings. Finally he was admitted to the mental asylum at St Rémy-de-

Provence in May 1889–May 1890 before shooting himself in July 1890 at the age of 37. This tortured, demented, genius decided he could face the brilliant, colourful Provençal life no longer.

Modern painters

Works by the two modern Provençal painters, Seyssaud and Chabaud, can be seen in the Musée des Beaux Arts in Marseille. Pablo Picasso lies buried in the seventeenth-century Château de Vauvenargues east of Aix which he owned, although most of his paintings were achieved on the Riviera coast. In the Réattu Museum of Arles is a donation of 57 of Picasso's drawings. The municipal museum of Bollène (in the NW of the Vaucluse) has an interesting collection of Picasso (and Chagall) drawings.

One of the strangest of the modern art painters is the Hungarian-born Victor Vasarely, born in 1908, a native of Gordes and Aix and a disciple of the modern Op Art producing optical illusions. To see these unusual *oeuvres*, visit the modern Vasarely *Musée didactique* in Gordes, or the Foundation Vasarely, Ave. Marcel-Pagnol in the western suburb of Aix.

The best museums in Provence in which to see the works of regional artists are:

Avignon	Calvet and Petit Palais
Aix	Granet, Atelier Cézanne
Arles	Réattu
Carpentras	Duplessis
Marseille	Beaux Arts and Cantini
Nîmes	Beaux Arts

They are usually closed on Tuesdays.

CHAPTER SEVEN:
THE FAR NORTH

North, NE and NW of Vaison-la-Romaine is a large area unknown to most visitors to Provence. This is in the hinterland east of the Rhône, the N6 and the great twin roads D158 and Autoroute de Soleil. The northern trio of towns are Grignan (Drome), Valréas and Nyons (Drome) situated in the old Enclave des Papes (of Avignon).

Grignan

This is in the Drome, and is a village (pop. 1,200) noted for its historical links with the elegant seventeenth-century Madame de Sevigné, who wrote so bewitchingly of Louis XIV court life and, by contrast, of her many sojourns in Grignan. The castle in which she lived was originally built in the eleventh-century and has been well restored since. The Louis XIII furnishings, grand staircase, Adhemar gallery, courtyard and superb views make a guided tour a pleasant occasion.

The collegiate sixteenth-century church of St Sauveur, twelfth-century town gate and belfry, a small museum, fountains and nearby grotto of Rochecourbière should be seen. There is a wine co-op (Caves du Tricastin) and the purple lavender beds produce a major crop. The Hôtel Sevigné is modest, tel. 75-46-50-97. There are a dozen small villages within easy reach. Taulignan (with thirteenth-century ramparts and fountains), Salles-sur-Bois (fourteenth- and fifteenth-century houses), Monbrison (castle of Pontaujard), Grillon (delightful village with hotel-restaurant La Truffe Noire, tel. 90-35-55-4l) and Chamaret (thirteenth-century watchtower).

Valréas

This is rather larger (pop. 9,000), situated in the Enclave des

Papes, a canton belonging to Vaucluse but geographically surrounded by the Drome department. King Charles VII stopped the rich, greedy Avignon popes buying up more land. The seventeenth-century Château de Simian, with its delicate frescoes, is partly the Hôtel de Ville, partly a museum, and very handsome it is too.

The eleventh-century Romanesque-Gothic church with a sixteenth-century organ, the chapel of the White Penitents, the old town with covered passages called *soustets*, towers, Renaissance houses and views of La Caronne River are all worth looking at. Streets lined with plane trees lead to a large wine co-op, the Caveau St Jean. Valréas owes much of its prosperity to carton manufacture, now the largest in France, dating from 1840. Lavender beds surround the town, truffles are grown locally and Valréas lambs feature on menus. Three modest hotels with restaurants are: La Camargue, tel. 90-35-01-51; La Paix, tel. 90-35-00-08; and Le Berteuil, tel. 90-35-01-30. The Tourist Board office is close to the Château in the Place A. Briand, tel. 90-35-04-71.

For five centuries, 23 June has seen a night-time procession called Petit St Jean, a historical pageant with *son et lumière* involving 300 characters. In July-August there is a festival with concerts, theatre and art exhibitions. Winter sees a *Santons* fair, and now there is a new carton museum. Valréas is surrounded by little wine villages with evocative names – St Pantaleon-des-Vignes, Rousset-les-Vignes, the oddly named Vinsobres (over 1,000 years old), Visan (fortified village with many beautiful old houses) and Richerenches (also a fortified village which was once a twelfth-century Knights Templar Commanderie).

Nyons

This town (pop. 6,300) is in the Drome bisected by the River Eygues. It has a medieval castle, and the seventh-century Saracen watchtower (now well restored) guarded the route (now the D94) which came westwards through the mountain ranges from Gap into the Tricastin plain. The old town has several *soustets*, many old houses, a fourteenth-century single span Romanesque bridge, lovely gardens and river views.

This is olive oil country, and in the town the Ramade Mill, Autrand Mill and Olive Oil Co-op in the Place Olivier de Serres offer guided tours for a small fee. The main sights are in the medieval Forts Quarter, 300 metres walk from the Tourist Office (Rue Sonays, tel. 80-6l-22-47). Do walk down the covered Rue des Grands Forts leading to the Church of St Vincent, past the thirteenth-century Tour Randonné, within which is the small chapel Notre Dame de Bon-Secours. It is an interesting, unspoilt town. Modest hotels include La Picholine, tel. 75-26-06-21, reached appropriately by the Promenade des Anglais. One French writer described Nyons as 'paradise on earth': well worth a stay. Local villages are Aubres beyond the gorge NE on the River Eygues, Mirabel (as pretty as it sounds) SW on the D538, and Venterol (with elegant sixteenth-century clocktower and pink-tiled old houses), NW sheltering in the lea of the Montagne des Vaux. The Grande Randonnée N9 crosses Nyons heading NW and SE respectively.

Bollène

SW of Valréas and west of Vaison are two more towns of interest. Bollène (pop. 12,500) is just east of the River Donzère, which has been harnessed here by the Compagnie Nationale du Rhône to provide electricity. Further up the Rhône valley is the Tricastin Nuclear Power Station (guided visits) and the famous thirteenth-century Pont-St-Esprit (pop. 8,000) with its old town 10 km west. Bollène sits on a hill, and despite the ultra-modern *barrages*, canals and power stations, has retained a ruined citadel, Museum Pasteur (closed Monday and Tuesday) with Chagall and Picasso drawings, the Pasteur gardens (the scientist stayed and worked in Bollène in 1882) and the twelfth-century collegiate church of St Martin. The Hotel du Lez, tel. 90-31-16-19 is inexpensive.

The Tourist Office is in Place Reynard de la Gardette, tel. 90-30-14-43, and will give you more information about the local northern sights which include the troglodyte village of Barry (4 km north) hewn into the hillside rocks, the castle of Mondragon, the citadel of Mornas, the village churches of St Restitut and La Garde Adhemar, the Templar tower at

Clansayes and, best of all, just north of Barry is St Paul-Trois-Châteaux (pop. 6,500). Although the castles have long since been cast down there is a lovely eleventh-century cathedral with frescoes and early mosaics. The town was known to the Romans as Augusta Tricastinorum and to the early Celts as Aeria. The local wine is Côtes de Tricastin.

Suze-la-Rousse

Inland from Bollène on the D994 for 16 km is the town of Suze-la-Rousse (pop. 1,500), which has two claims to fame. There is a well restored castle, originally a hunting lodge of the Princes of Orange (visits in the afternoons July-August), which now houses the major University of Wine, which is the town's other big attraction. As the name implies, the castle, sixteenth-century parsonage, the chapel of St-Sebastion and the cornhall market are built of red stone. In July a pageant called Nuits Feodales takes place. The place to stay is the Relais du Château, tel. 75-04-87-07, which has a good restaurant.

Neighbouring villages

Villages nearby include Rochegude in the south, whose castle harbours a first-class restaurant; La Baume-de-Transit in the north with a very old watchtower. Together with neighbouring Montsegur-sur-Lauzon, these are the truffle capitals of the region. Finally there is Bouchet, with a Romanesque church and a Cistercian abbey where Côtes du Rhône wines are ageing gracefully in oak barrels.

A.T.M. Voyages, 15 Place Castil-Blaze, 84302 Cavaillon, tel. 90-71-37-66, offer a two-day wine-tasting tour from 1580 francs. This includes a visit to the Wine University, to the cellars of Vinsobres, vineyards of Gigondas etc. Tours start and end in Avignon. Provence Voyages, 3 Bd. Raspail, 84000 Avignon, tel. 90-82-08-46, offer another wine tour to Suze-la-Rousse, Beaumes-de-Venise, Tavel and Lirac from 1215 francs.

CHAPTER EIGHT:
VAISON-LA-ROMAINE

When the Romans conquered the Ligurians and the Voconces from Vacio Vocontiorum it was, even then, a civilised Celtic regional capital. The River Ouvèze, flowing from the Alps to link up with the Rhône and Sorgue, bisects Vaison, so that two quite disparate little towns face each other across the river.

The Roman influence

On the north side the Romans had built a considerable colony for wealthy administrators, officers of the legions and merchants, with a theatre, temples, villas and usual market place (now clearly revealed). On the south side atop a steep hill is the ramparted Haute Ville, with a château built mainly in the twelfth century as a refuge. Urbs Opulentissima, the Roman town, was sacked on their departure by the Barbarians, with Visigoths and Ostrogoths amongst them. The two cities, the old Roman (the mini-Pompeii) and the medieval, are linked by a fine single-arched Pont Romain across the Ouvèze.

Although Vaison has none of the outstanding Roman antiquities as do such towns as Arles, Orange or Nîmes, it is one of the most interesting and informative archaeological sites of the Roman world in Europe. Some of the original Vaison marbles are in the British Museum.

Vaison now has a population of nearly 6,000, and fortunately it is off the beaten track, being roughly equidistant from Carpentras, Orange, Nyons and Valréas. But its reputation as an attractive town with superb Roman antiquities means that the tourist coaches roll in during the summer months. Moreover, the famous wine growing areas to the SW and NW make it an ideal town in which to base oneself for a few days' holiday.

Tourist information

The Tourist Office is in the Place du Chanoine Sautel, tel. 90-36-02-11, a few metres away from the Roman Puymin Quarter (Messius' house, Pompey's portico, Nymphaeum, villas, theatre and museum) and across the road the Villasse Quarter (Dolphin house, basilica, shopping streets, Patrician's house) in Colonnade Street. A ticket costs 17 francs for a guided visit. The Maison du Vin has a large office below ground next to the Tourist Office with maps, guides and information about all the wine châteaux and co-ops within a radius of 50 km.

Any budding archaeological student can book three-or-five day practical courses on the Roman antiquities through A.P.R.A.V., 4 Rue St Charles, 84000 Avignon, tel. 90-86-33-33. There are 'stages' i.e. courses at Vaison and Rasteau (10 km west). Guided tours of the Antiquities are made by lecturers of the National Historical Monument Bureau (C.N.M.H.S.).

On the same side of the river as the Roman sites is the very handsome Cathedral of Notre Dame, dating from the sixth century when St Quentin was Bishop. His sarcophagus, bishop's throne, altar, cloisters and chapel should be seen. The cloister has a small museum of early Christian art. The main town museum is in the Roman Puymin quarter and contains most of the finds discovered by Abbot Sautel during the excavations he directed from 1907-50.

The Haute Ville

Across the river, by the modern bridge, opposite the cathedral is the medieval Haute Ville, now much restored, with cobbled streets and fountains. Look for the Rue des Fours (ovens), Rue de l'Horloge, Place du Vieux Marché and Rue de l'Evêche. The twelfth-century castle on the top is still sadly ruined and empty, but has superb views towards Mont

Ventoux and the Ouvèze valley and, of course, the Roman town below and across the river.

The best hotel-restaurant is Le Beffroi in the Haute Ville, but there are half a dozen budget hotels including Burrhus, L'Escargot d'Or, Platanes, Théâtre Romain, Les Voconces and La Piscine. For restaurants, try Les Voconces, Place de Montfort where a three-course meal including *salade camarguaise, filet de loup* (fish!) *à la crème et aux fines herbes* costs 49 francs. At La Grasihado the 56-franc menu includes *salade paysanne* and *côte de porc provençale*.

Festivals of Vaison

For a small town, Vaison has much to offer. In February is held the Tuesday morning Asparagus fair of St-Quenin; in May (Pentecost) the Corso (street processions and floats); in June on Tuesday mornings are the lime fruit markets and July—August the choral and folklore gala festivals. Finally in November is the fair of St André to taste the *vins primeurs*.

Touring

Excursions from Vaison are numerous. NE, east and SE are mountain ranges and river valleys with dozens of little villages to explore. One could spend a week quite happily driving, cycling or walking in the Mont Ventoux range. The Grandes Randonnées, GR91, GR91b, GR9, GR4, thread their way west to east. Objectives might include the villages of Buis-les-Baronnie, Mollans-sur-Ouvèze, Malaucène and Sault.

Sault

Few British tourists have discovered little Sault (pop. 1,250) tucked away 40 km east of Carpentras and surrounded by lavender fields. To its south is the plateau of Vaucluse, to its immediate west the Gorges de Nesque and to the NW the mountains of Ventoux. This little health resort sits happily on a small hill between the River Nesque and the Croc in the plateau d'Albion, with six minor roads feeding into it. Sturdy walkers using the GR91, GR4 and GR9 can reach Sault from the west, but the most spectacular approach is by the D942/D1 from Carpentras.

Originally known as Saltus, this old Celtic town has many early archeological finds deposited in the local museum (closed Wednesday) situated above the library. The twelfth-century church of St Sauveur has a remarkable nave, and the remains of the eleventh-century castle, medieval streets and houses are well worth a visit. Two modest hotels are Le Provençal, tel. 90-64-01-25 and Signoret, tel. 90-64-00-45. The Tourist Office is open only in season, tel. 90-64-01-21. The point about Sault (noted for its nougat) is that it is an excellent excursion centre for Mont Ventoux, the Nesque Gorges and Haute Provence. Organised walks, pot holing, ski-ing and horse riding activities are locally available. The lavender and honey villages of Aurel and Ferrassières to the North and St Christol to the SE are within easy range, but the main sights are the spectacular gorges and hills on the western flank.

Touring

A full day-round tour starting from Sault would head north on the D942 past the curious *aven* to Aurel and Gour des Oules. Then go west on the D72 through Reilhanette, D41 under the Col des Aires to little Brantes. Stop here for a moment and take photographs of its old castle against the huge bulk of the Ventoux range perched above the Toulourenc River. Brantes is an artisan centre, with pottery and earthenware, weaving and local ironwork. There is even a little hotel-restaurant, L'Auberge, tel. 75-28-01-68. Keep on the D72, parallel to the River Derbous, to the T-junction with the D5, west to Pierre-longue with its perched church, to Mollans sur Ouvèze (pop. 700) with bridge and belfry. You can continue into Vaison or side-slip south via Entrechaux on the D13. An ideal place for lunch is the Hôtel la Nanescale, tel. 90-36-23-80, because on the menu will be truffles, local fruit, vegetables, goat's cheese and AOC Côtes du Ventoux wine! That's not all. Look at the romantic ruins of the medieval castle, a fourteenth-century bridge and lovely machicolated fourteenth-century town gates.

Keep south on the D13 to join the D938 into Malaucène (pop. 2,000). Pope Clement V erected the fourteenth-century church with its historic organ, and the little Chapel of Notre-Dame-du-Grozeau dates from the twelfth century. There are remains of a château, fifteenth-century clocktower and eighteenth-century hospital. Malaucène has good local fishing, ski-ing and organised climbs on Mont Ventoux. A curiosity is that potatoes were first grown in Provence in this little town. The local honey, goat's cheese and wine can be tasted at the Hôtel l'Origan, tel. 90-65-27-08, or Le Cours, tel. 90-65-20-31, both in the Course des Isnards. The Tourist Office is in the Ave. de Verdun, tel. 90-65-22-59. I refrain from making a joke about visiting little Suzette, snuggling at the foot of the hill of St Amand, which is the highest of the peaks of Les Dentelles de Montmirail (height 750 metres) a few km west of Malaucène. A lovely climb via a G.R. or the winding D90, and you will gather that this little town is an ideal family holiday centre (for the active) with campsites and seven restaurants!

There is now a choice of route. Either take the mountain road, the D974 via Mont Serein, Mont Ventoux itself (about 2,000 metres high) and Le Chalet-Reynard (popular ski resort) — about 30 km of very winding road with fabulous views — or follow the more leisurely southern route D938, D19 and D974. This will take you through Bedoin (pop. 1,800), a medieval village with ochre-coloured houses, a seventeenth-century Jesuit church and an eleventh-century chapel, of Ste Madeleine. The hotels are L'Escapade, Place du Portail de l'Olivier, tel. 90-65-60-21 and La Brechette, tel. 90-65-60-96. The Tourist Office is open in season, tel. 90-65-63-95. Bedoin is a popular little village with seven restaurants, five campsites and a nudist colony! Both alternative routes link up and the last 20 km on the D164 is SE back into Sault.

One last word. Either based on Sault or Vaison (or temptations on the way), this circuit is the real, genuine old Provence of hills, rivers, medieval villages, wine and honey, lavender, truffles and goat's cheese — and superlative photogenic sights all day long!

CHAPTER NINE:
CARPENTRAS AND CAVAILLON

Carpentras, the third town in the Vaucluse, lies halfway between Cavaillon and Orange at the intersection of the D950, D938, D942 and D974. It is a prosperous town which is rarely visited by British tourists: this is a pity because, as the former capital of the Comtat Venaissin where the rector or administrator lived, Carpentras is a flourishing town with 25,000 inhabitants.

The history of Carpentras

Situated near the River Auzon on the crossroads to Orange, Vaison, Mont Ventoux, Cavaillon and Avignon, Carpentras has always been a market town. Various food specialities include Berlingots sweets, fruits and vegetables of all kinds and truffles. The local wines of Côtes du Ventoux can be tasted in the local cave co-ops. Six centuries BC the Greeks and Phoceans came here to buy corn, honey, goats, sheep and their skins. Carpentras horses and appropriate chariots (Karpenton = Carpentras) were also much sought after. The original inhabitants were a Celtic tribe, the Meminiens. The Romans colonised Carpentras and the Forum Neronis (Nero was Julius Caesar's general) and the Arc de Triomphe are visible legacies. The latter was built in the first century to celebrate Augustus' victory over the Barbarians and is now called Porte d'Orange. Curiously enough it was Pope Clement V, in 1316, who settled in Carpentras and died there the following year. On his death the Cardinals fled to Avignon and the next Pope was installed there in 1316.

The Tourist Office is at 170 Allées Jean-Jaurès, tel. 90-63-00-78, a long boulevard lined with plane trees on the east side of town and a few minutes' walk from the huge Hôtel-Dieu (closed Saturday-Sunday), an eighteenth-century hospital. There is an old pharmacy, chapel, and magnificent staircase to see (look for the funny monkey paintings!).

Carpentras is one of several Provençal towns offering sanctuary in the Middle Ages to the Jewish community, and the synagogue dates from 1367 (although it was much restored in the eighteenth and twentieth centuries) and claims to be the oldest in France. It is situated close to the Hôtel de Ville. A guided tour takes three-quarters of an hour, but not at weekends, and the oven for unleavened bread and purification baths should be noted. Up to the Revolution, the Jewish colony numbered 1,200 and in the fourteenth century financed the Avignon Popes.

Two hundred metres away, in a cluster of buildings, is the Gothic Cathedral of St Siffrein with an historic organ and Jews' Gate built in 1405, but with twelfth-century Romanesque vestiges. Many Avignon painters' works can be seen, including Mignard, Parrocel, and Duplessis. Next door is the seventeenth-century Palais de Justice and the Roman Porte d'Orange.

The sights of Carpentras

Rather surprisingly, Carpentras has no less than six fine museums (all closed on Tuesday). The outstanding Inguimbertine library is housed in the eighteenth-century Hôtel d'Allemand in the Boulevard Albin Durand on the western boulevard. Nearly a quarter of a million fine old tomes, manuscripts, illuminated Books of Hours, and 200 very early printed books (including a rare Petrarch) were assembled together by Malachie d'Inguimbert, Bishop of Carpentras from 1735–57, plus later additions. In the same complex is the Musée Duplessis with Provençal primitives and later schools (including Parrocels, Vernet, Rigaud and Duplessis). The Musée Comtadin nearby is devoted to folklore, arts and local history. Three more museums are a few hundred metres away – the Sobirats (*faiences* and furnishings), Rue de College;

Lapidaire (archeological and natural history), Rue des Stes Maries; and in the Cathedral of St Siffrein is housed the Treasury (St Mors bridle and bit made of nails from the Cross) and Museum of Sacred Art. Uniquely there is a poetry museum in the Parc des Ombrages, Route de Pernes, of ancient, contemporary and modern poetry.

Other sights are the seventeenth-century Chapel of Notre Dame de Santé, La Charité (a poorhouse built in 1669 and now a cultural centre), a seventeenth-century College Chapel, sixteenth-century belltower and eighteenth-century aqueduct to the east side of the town. There are a score of seventeenth- and eighteenth-century town mansions to be seen in the Rue Moricelly, Rue de la Monnaie, Place St Siffrein and Place Ste Marthe. Local tours are arranged each day by the Tourist Office during the season. The annual fair is held on 27 November when the St Mors relic is shown. The weekly *Grand Marché* is held on Thursday mornings. The winter truffle market is also held on Thursday mornings in the Place Aristide-Briand. The summer festival takes place in July-August, and a great procession occurs at the beginning of July. Grand Prix horse racing events are at Easter and in July.

Carpentras has a number of tourist circuits and these are:-

1. South to Pernes-les-Fontaines, La Roque-sur-Pernes, Saumane, Fontaine-de-Vaucluse and L'Isle-sur-la-Sorgue — total about 50 km.
2. SE to St Didier, Le Beaucet, Venasque, L'Abbaye de Senanque, Gordes and Murs — about 70 km.
3. Another circuit is east to Mazon, Malemort-du-Comtat, Blauvac, Méthamis, Sault, Monieux, Villes-sur-Auzon and Mormoiron — altogether 93 km.
4. Or NE to St Pierre-de-Vassols, Modène, Crillon-le-Brave, Bédoin, Chalet Reynard, top of Ventoux Hills to Mont Serein, Malaucène and Caromb — a distance of 80 km.
5. Finally a northern circuit — Aubignon, Beaumes-de-Venise, Vacqueyras, Gigondas, Les Dentelles-de-Montmirail, Sablet, Seguret, Vaison-la-Romaine, Malaucène, Suzette, Lafare, La Roque-Airie and Le Barroux — a really interesting tour of 74 km.

Carpentras hotels and restaurants

The best hotels in Carpentras are Le Safari or L'Univers, and budget hotels are Le Cours, Bd. A. Durand, tel. 90-63-10-07 and almost next door, Le Théâtre, tel. 90-63-02-90. La Lavande, Bd. A Rogier, tel. 90-63-13-49 is also good value. One eats well and inexpensively at L'Univers, tel. 90-63-00-05, at Le Marijo, Rue Raspail or Les Halles, Place Galonne. We had a good 49-franc meal at the Coq Hardi. Writing of food, however, a good present to bring back with you are some of the traditional sweets, Olives de Provence, which are coloured green and black and contain almond paste. Others are shaped and coloured like wine corks. Calissons d'Aix are made by Leonard Parli, and Nougat de Sault by André Boyer (since 1887). The Berlingots are made by Hardy of Carpentras. Croquettes Aujoras are Provençal biscuits with almond flavouring.

Parking

Two final reminiscences about Carpentras. Hundreds of smart new black bollards deter the car-parker, but nevertheless we found it easy to park in Carpentras, unlike Aix or Nîmes. And there are still some of those old-fashioned stonewalled but practical, outside gentlemen's W.C.'s, where only trousers and heads can be discerned!

En route to Cavaillon

Half an hour's drive south on the D938, parallel to the canal de Carpentras, is another major bustling Provençal town, in many ways similar in style. Cavaillon is not a town that many tourists visit, but it is the key to the fertile Coulon valley lying between the Montagne Luberon and the high Plateau de Vaucluse.

Pernes-les-Fontaines

On the D938 south to Cavaillon are two towns that should on no account be missed. Pernes-les-Fontaines (pop. 7,000) prospers on its fruit farms (melons, cherries, grapes and strawberries) and as its name implies is well watered since the

River Nesque flows gently through the centre. There are 32 fountains scattered around the narrow streets. Take your pick but the Cormorant in Rue Raspail is as elegant as you could hope for. The town ramparts are well preserved with fortified gates and towers. The Notre-Dame sixteenth-century tower, linking the bridge and chapel, is enchanting. The twelfth-century Ferrande Tower is decorated with the oldest frescoes in Provence. They were painted in about 1275 and include one of a horseback fight between Moor and Christian and another of Pope Clement IV investing Charles of Anjou with the Kingdom of Naples in 1266. (There are guided tours to see this quadrangular crenellated building.) Also see the Comtes de Toulouse castle keep and the Notre-Dame de Nazareth church built over a crypt, with its historic organ. The Tourist Office, tel. 90-61-31-04, arranges guided tours. Besides fishing in the Nesque, there is a flying club, hunting and rough riding events. Two hotels are the Prato Plage, tel. 90-66-51-41 and L'Hermitage, tel. 90-66-51-41. If you do not know about Pernes you will be tempted to miss it as the main road tends to bypass the town.

L'Isle-sur-la-Sorgue

Known as the 'Comtadine Venice', L'Isle-sur-la-Sorgue (pop. 12,000) lies 17 km south of Pernes. It is criss-crossed with canals and five tributaries of the River Sorgue. There are a number of large water wheels and water power helps the local quilt and rug artisan factories. The seventeenth-century church has rich wood panelling and gold decorations with paintings and frescoes by the Provençal painters Mignard and Parrocel. See also the seventeenth-century hospital, fountains and Renaissance houses. The Place de la Juiverie indicates that the Jewish community were given sanctuary here (as in Carpentras and Cavaillon). The Sorgue festival takes place in July, with water jousting and horse races. The Tourist Office is in Place de l'Eglise, tel. 90-38-04-78. The excellent local fish include eel, trout and crayfish. There are several modest hotels including Le Cours, tel. 90-38-01-18, St Martin, tel. 90-38-05-16 and Le Vieux Isle, tel. 90-38-00-46.

Cavaillon

Four centuries BC, the Celtic tribe of the Cabellio were trading with the Massilia Greeks of Marseille. Almost certainly they were selling sweet rosy-pink melons, since Cavaillon is the melon capital of France. About 200,000 tons are grown in the fertile plains watered by the Rivers Durance and Coulon. Before the Romans came in 42 BC, the ferrymen in their leather coracles transferred goods and people across the river and for over a thousand years took them the 30 km NW to the confluence of the Durance and the Rhône south of Avignon.

Now a busy agricultural market town of 21,000 people, Cavaillon has five major roads feeding into it, whilst the Autoroute A7 carries the Avignon-Salon-Marseille traffic on the westerly bank of the river.

The only Roman site is a small arch incorporated in the church wall of St Veran. The cloisters and historic organ of the twelfth-century Cathedral of St Veran and a superb eighteenth-century synagogue with delicate iron tracery and sculpted woodwork are worth visiting. The Cathedral has paintings by Parrocel and Mignard (open mornings only). The Synagogue in the Rue Hebraique (closed Tuesday) has a Jewish Comtat Venaissin Museum, although the Jewish community was much smaller than that of Carpentras. The Archeological Museum in the Grand Rue (closed Tuesday, guided visits) has a collection of funeral urns, Roman and Gallic coins, pottery and mementoes of the Hôtel-Dieu hospital. The Tourist Office is in Rue Saunerie, tel. 90-71-32-01. A walk on the west side of town to the calvary on the top of St Jacques hill gives you nearly 360° views of the Durance valley, Mont Ventoux, the Luberon and the plain of Cavaillon with its market gardens. There is a St Veran fair, an Ascension procession to the Calvary, St Gilles festival (first Monday in September) and horse-racing events in May and September.

The best hotel is the Christel and budget hotels are Le Grenouillet, 133 Ave. Berthelot, tel. 90-78-08-08, and Le Provence, tel. 90-78-03-38.

CHAPTER TEN:
GORDES

One of the best known, prettiest Provençal hill villages, with a population of 1,600, Gordes is situated halfway between Cavaillon and Apt, 400 metres up the heights of the Vaucluse plateau overlooking the River Imergue to the south. It is dominated by a fine fourteenth-century Renaissance Château where once an eleventh-century fortress stood. Two huge round machicolated towers are twelfth- and thirteenth-century and give the impression of great military strength. The village was badly damaged by the retreating Germans in 1944. Fortunately Gordes has been carefully renovated, mainly by a colony of artists (as has Oppede-le-Vieux, another *village perché* 10 km south). The castle houses the provocative Vasarely Museum (closed Tuesdays). The painter, Victor Vasarely, leased the château from the village council for 33 years at a peppercorn rent of 1 franc a year. In all there are 1,500 paintings, scores of brilliantly coloured tapestries and it is well worth 10 francs to see the works of the father of kinetic art. The village church of St Firmin, with a historic organ, was built in 1704. The Tourist Office is open only in season, at Place du Château, tel. 90-72-02-75. The village is so photogenic and attractive, with its old stone houses tiered up the hillside below the castle, that hotel prices are quite high. The best hotel is the Domaine de l'Enclos but the small Hostellerie Provençale, Place du Château, tel. 90-72-01-07 is relatively inexpensive. A good reason for staying at Gordes is that half a dozen interesting and varied sights are close at hand.

Senanque

Senanque Abbey was founded in 1148 by the Cistercian Order and is 3 km north set in a lonely valley. The cloister with its arcades, chapter house, monks' dormitory and abbey church should be visited. Surrounded by old oak trees and lavender beds, the Senanque has many activities. It has an Institute for Medieval Studies, a Saharan Toureg museum, concerts of Gregorian music, art exhibitions and is inundated in mid-summer by visitors.

Bories

The village of Bories is 3 km SW off the D2. At the end of the 2 km winding track is a small museum showing the traditional rural lifestyle. We counted about 45 of these loaf-shaped hut-houses (called *bories*, hence the village name), made of large stones and cantilevered roofs. No mortar is used and they are classic dry-stone dwelling places. Experts differ as to the age of these strange remote buildings. They are set close together and were unlikely to be shepherds' huts. In any case they are large enough to house, rather uncomfortably, a dozen inhabitants. Their design is certainly pre-Roman, probably Celtic Ligurian, of 2,500 years ago. But they are so well preserved that they were probably 'assembled' in the seventeenth-century, possibly by town dwellers fleeing from the plague. The three thousand *bories* are to be found all over the Savournin plateau within a 20-km radius of Gordes and Murs to the NE.

Fontaine-de-Vaucluse

The Fontaine-de-Vaucluse, 5 km west of Gordes, was the spiritual home of the poet Petrarch. He met his heroine Laura at the Eglise des Cordeliers in Avignon in April 1327 and composed 366 poems of devotion to her. For nearly twenty years he stayed near the château at the head of the valley of the River Sorgue, which wells up from a deep black pool at the foot of high cliffs. If you can brave the tourist traps, walk along the river banks to see the fountain emerging from a cavern (sometimes the water gushes out at the rate of 150,000 litres per second!). A million visitors come here each year to see one of the natural wonders of Provence.

The local Hôtel des Sources, tel. 90-20-31-84, is reasonable. From 15 June to 15 September there is a 'Son et lumière' spectacle. The Tourist Office in the village is open only in season, tel. 90-20-32-22.

Venasque

To the north of Gordes are the gorges and forest of Venasque. The picturesque village is perched on a rocky crag overlooking the River Nesque and has two ancient buildings: the fifth- to sixth-century square baptistry of the Notre-Dame church and, 2½ km north, the Notre-Dame-de-la-Vie chapel with a remarkable tomb, dating from 604 AD, of Bishop Bohetius of Carpentras.

Other places to visit

West of Venasque are Pernes-les-Fontaines and L'Isle-sur-la-Sorgue on the Carpentras-Cavaillon road.

Five km south of Gordes is the stained glass museum (Musée du Vitrail), next door on the D148 to a medieval olive oil mill owned by Frédérique Duran, a lady artist specialising in stained glass tiles. The artists' colony exhibit and sell their work at the Moulin des Bouillons.

To the east of Gordes is the village of Roussillon (pop. 1,300) where there is an artists' colony, which has an 'Ochre' festival for three days over Ascension. The ochre rock is quarried in this region and many of the houses are built of one or more of 16 or 17 different red-carmine-scarlet-ochre stones. Try the Hôtel Residence des Ocres, Route de Gordes, tel. 90-75-60-50.

Lastly, for energetic walkers visiting the region, the Grandes Randonnées 91 and 6 pass close by Gordes.

CHAPTER ELEVEN:
APT AND PERTUIS

Nobody could call Apt an impressive town, but it is ideal for anyone wishing for a base from which to explore the high plateau of the Vaucluse to the north or the hills and National Park of the Luberon to the south. The N100 from Avignon to Digne passes west to east through Apt (pop. 12,500), which bestrides the River Calavon.

Local history

Before the Romans arrived in 50 BC, the local tribe were the Vulgientes, and that of the region the Albizi or Albiens (from which came the name Albion, as in perfidious!). It became the Roman colonia Apta Julia in honour of Julius Caesar who passed through it after his Spanish campaigns. The only traces now of their four centuries of rule are the baths under the sub-prefecture buildings, the crypt in the old cathedral and part of the arena underneath the museum (which in turn contains many Roman finds — coins, oil lamps, sarcophagi and mosaics). As elsewhere in Provence, there followed five centuries of barbaric invasions — Alamans, Francs in 276, the Burgondes, Visigoths, Ostrogoths, Francs in the fifth century, Lombards from northern Italy, Saxons in the sixth century and Saracens in the ninth century. Luckily the town inhabitants found refuge in the hills to the north or south. On Easter Day 776, Charlemagne consecrated the new cathedral and 'discovered' in a crypt the body of the Virgin's mother.

On the last Sunday in July the annual pilgrimage takes place. This is dedicated to St Anne, mother of the Virgin, whose body (legend has it) had been originally brought to Apt from Marseille. The shroud of St Anne, along with many other eleventh- to thirteenth-century manuscripts, reliquaries and treasures brought back from the First Crusade are to be seen in the treasury and sacristy in the eleventh-century cathedral of St Anne (closed Monday, Saturday and Sunday afternoons). It is in the centre of the old town which lies on the south bank of the river. In 1660 Queen Anne of Austria came on a pilgrimage to the town and the royal chapel was built to commemorate her visit (as mother of Louis XIV, born in 1638).

Plague decimated Apt in 1348 and in 1720. The wars of religion also took their toll since the region was deeply involved in the 'Heresy of the Vaudois'. Pierre de Vaux founded the brotherhood called the 'Poor of Lyon' in 1179, who were then called after him, the Vaudois. In 1332 the Avignon Popes decreed this sect to be heretics and eventually, by the Merindo Act of 1540, the heretics were all sentenced to torture and death. The villages SW of Apt, including Merindol, Cadenet and Oppede, were all dedicated to this quite harmless sect (who believed in Communion and the baptism of adults but not other Catholic precepts). Twenty-two villages were exterminated and over 2,000 Vaudois slaughtered. Soon the wars of religion escalated and next the Huguenots were expelled from the region and Apt was besieged in 1560, 1562 and 1586 (the massacre of St Bartholomew took place in 1572). As if in retribution for all this pointless slaughter, plague ravaged the region from 1581-1589.

During the French Revolution, a score of 'notables' were guillotined. Apt was fortunate, although the *citoyens* vandalised many chapels in the town.

Now, thanks to its local trade in preserved fruits, mushrooms, lavender crops, ceramics, ochre refining, burnished copper products and tourism, Apt has become prosperous.

Places of interest

The Tourist Office, tel. 90-74-03-18, is in the Place Bouquerie, on the south side of the main bridge and N100, opposite the Mairie, and Sous-prefecture. Guided tours of the old town are on Wednesdays in season or on request from groups. Besides the cathedral and the museum, the eighteenth-century Episcopal palace, and sixteenth-century clock tower should be seen. The main market takes place on Saturday morning — masses of candied fruits, cherries in season, and local wines. The large public gardens are east of the Cours Lauze de Perret on the east side of town. The best hotel is Le Ventoux, 67 Ave. Victor Hugo and the two budget hotels are Le Relais de Roquefure, tel. 90-74-22-80 and du Palais, 12 Place Gabriel-Peri, tel. 90-74-00-54. For restaurants, try Le Jardin des Cafés, 16 Place Jean-Jaurès or La Terrine Gourmande, Rue de la République.

Before you leave Apt try the candied fruits and visit the factory at Aptunion (3.30 p.m. in July-August) on the N100, tel. 90-74-10-55 or Clerici, Route de Buoux (opposite Gendarmerie) tel. 90-74-09-95, and the artists' colony, with Hostellerie la Paradon, tel. 90-68-04-05.

Touring

Excursions north of the town can be made to Gargas (the old château is now the *mairie*), Villars, and St Saturnin (château, ramparts and priory). To the SW is Bonnieux (Romanesque church, thirteenth-century towers and ramparts). M. Pinater (a wine grower of repute) is the owner of the Domaine de l'Isolette on the D3. West of Bonnieux is the château of Lacoste (tel. M. Bouer on 90-75-80-39) which once was defended by the persecuted Vaudois against the Catholic troops. Rather later the de Sade family owned it, and at the Revolution it was pillaged, but is now admirably restored.

West of Apt on the N10 is Goult (a notable priory, scene of an annual pilgrimage, Romanesque church, chapel and château). The Cave Co-op de Lumières is open in mid-summer only, to sell Côtes de Ventoux and Côtes du Luberon wines. The co-op in Bonnieux is in the *quartier de la gare*, tel. 90-75-80-03. Three km east of Gault is the famous Roman Pont Julien on the Via Domitia, with three arches said to date from the third century BC.

South of Apt is the château of Buoux known as Le Fort, and Priory of St Symphorien. To the SE is Saignon (abbey of St Eusebe, a Romanesque church with reliquary of the Cross).

In the NE sector are the huge ochre quarries off the D22, about 11 km from Apt, called the Colorado de Rustrel, and Simiane with château, a twelfth-century medieval keep (La Rotonde) and an old village of character.

On these travels one can eat well and inexpensively in Gargas (La Campagne or Moulin de Lavon), Saignon (Beausejour on Route de Digne) and Rustrel (Le Rustreou).

The Regional Nature Park of the Luberon

Created in 1977, an area of 130,000 hectares (300,000 acres) has been designated as a special nature park. About 85,000 inhabitants of 51 communes live in the park, which includes the area around Apt in the north, and stretches to Cavaillon in the west, the area with Pertuis and 'pays d'Aigues' in the south, and east towards Manosque. The office administering the park is the Maison du Parc, 1 Place Jean-Jaurès, 84400 Apt, tel. 90-74-08-55. There you can get information about nature walks, and rambles, wildlife studies, exhibitions, special museums (paleontology, local history), visits to the stone bories at Viens, the ochre mines at Roussillon, the cedar forest of Petit Luberon, wine tastings and visits. The Château de Buouy organises 'green' classes and studies.

For two thousand years the area of the Luberon and its neighbour, the mountain range of Ventoux, was a sanctuary for the persecuted. Celtic druids hid from the Romans. Everybody hid from the Barbarians, Vandals, Visigoths and the northern seaborne invaders. This is hermit country and there are probably still some living rough if you look closely. Refugees for cause de religion came here – the wretched Vaudois, Albigensians and Huguenots, bourgeois refugees from the French Revolution and Resistance maquis in the Second World War hiding from the revolting SS and Wehrmacht – they all sought shelter in the caves, grottoes, bories and woods.

79

The Montagne du Luberon is divided into two parts — Le Petit Luberon to the west which includes the villages of Oppede-le-Vieux (artists' colony), Menerbes (citadel and fourteenth-century church), Lacoste (Sade family) and Bonnieux (ramparts, twelfth-century church, bakery museum in the Rue de la République and Hôtel César, Place de la Liberté, tel. 90-75-80-18). The D943 south from Apt towards Pertuis bisects the Luberon. On the east side there is Le Grand Luberon which includes the villages of Lourmarin (château with guided visit) and artists' colony, with Hostellerie lou Paradou, tel. 90-68-04-05. There is also Cucuron (Marc Deydier Luberon museum, Romanesque church Notre-Dame-de-Beaulieu with historic organ, and Hôtel l'Arbre de Mai, tel. 90-77-25-11) and Ansouis, which offers the Sabran castle from the tenth century with a guided tour (one of the best in Provence), the 'Extraordinary' Museum, opened in 1975, (closed Tuesday) and the Rue du Vieux Moulin furnished in Provençal style with free entrance. The artisan activities are of a high standard and there is also a wine Co-op. The Grand Luberon continues to the east on the D27 past the Etang de la Bonde, La Motte d'Aigues on the D42 to Vitrolles.

Touring

From Apt there are two good tours, SW to Le Petit Luberon or SE to Le Grand Luberon, both taking between three and four hours. From Ansouis on the D56 it is a short distance to Pertuis and I have listed below a few of the artisans worth a visit on your travels in the surrounding region.

● La Tour d'Aigues

Christian Bellamy paints on silk *(Peinture sur soie)* and Michel Pellegrin is a noted local painter. Gilles Avenard works with silk, cotton and wool and Monique Labarthe is a potter.

● La Bastidonne

M. Quidort, an *apiculteur*, has won a Paris medal for his fine honey.

● **Beaumont de Pertuis**

M. Lemetter is a *sculpteur ceramiste*.

● **La Motte d'Aigues**

M. Dupont owns the Catido pottery and Madame Delattre is the local painter.

● **Grambois**

There are many artisans. Pierre Graille claims to be the *meilleur ouvrier de France* as a santon-maker, *faiencier*, painter and sculptor! You will find painters, ironworkers, wood-turners and honey growers, as well as the Cave Co-op des Coteaux (closed Tuesdays), tel. 90-77-92-04.

● **La Bastide des Jourdans**

M. Christophe paints with watercolours, oils and on silk. The Mijo pottery runs courses and Nichole de la Bastide makes *faience* work. There are two small hotels: Le Mirvy, tel. 90-77-83-23 and Cheval Blanc, tel. 90-77-81-08, both offering *cuisine gourmande*.

Pertuis

In the valley of the canal de Cadanet (which runs parallel to the River Durance) sits the quite undistinguished town of Pertuis. It has a population of 12,000 and lies on the crossroads of the routes from Marseille to the Alps and from Avignon to the Gorges du Verdon. Its history is also undistinguished! The old town has a ruined castle, a fortified fourteenth-century clocktower and the church of St Nicholas, the tourist office is in the place Mira Beau next door to St Nicholas tel. 90-79-15-56. There, they organise guided tours within and without the town.

Despite this, Pertuis has one virtue — it is in the right place! Close to the Luberon range of hills (villages of Cadenet, Lourmarin, Cucuron, Ansouis, La Tour d'Aigues) there are many wine co-ops (cellier de Marrenon at the last named); many châteaux to see (Cadanet where Napoleon's drummer

81

boy, who helped beat the Austrians, lived, Châteaurenard, Tour d'Aigues, La Roque d'Antheron); churches and abbeys (Silvacane abbey now well restored to its twelfth-century glory, Noves Romanesque church, the Chartreuse de Bonpas, Rognes seventeenth-century church); natural beauties (panorama at Châteaurenard, forest of Pelicier, ochre cliffs, Gorges of Regalon), and unnatural beauties (the St Christopher reservoir, near Rognes and the huge power stations of St Esteve, Mallemort and Jouques).

Moreover, the hotels in Pertuis are inexpensive: des Cornarel, 24 Rue de la Tour, tel. 90-79-14-34; du Cours, 100 Place Jean-Jaurès, tel. 90-79-00-68. Restaurants include the du Cours, Le 4 Septembre, and L'Aubarestio. For 56 francs the Grand Café Thomas, Place Jean-Jaurès have a three-course meal including *crudités*, *lapin braisé*, *fromage* or dessert.

In May Pertuis has a *grande foire*, in early June street processions i.e. a *corso*, and another on the last weekend in October/beginning of November. Market day is on Friday.

CHAPTER TWELVE:
AIX-EN-PROVENCE

Plutarch recorded that when the Roman general Marius defeated the Barbarians near Aix in 102 BC, over 100,000 Cimbri and Teutons were slain and the little River Arc ran scarlet with blood after the two battles. Twenty-three years before that carnage the Roman consul, Sextius Calvinus, founded a thermal spa station and named it after himself, Aquae Sextiae, having conquered the local tribe of Salyans based on neighbouring Entremont. The twenty-one sparkling fountains are scattered around the old town and the thermal baths, appropriately in the Cours Sextius, still offer solace and comfort two thousand years later.

Local history

When Julius Caesar sacked Massilia, Aquae (or Aix) became a Roman colony and later capital of Gallia Narbonensis Secunda. The town became an Archbishopric in the fifth century after the Romans left but in 574 AD was sacked by the Lombards. Its influence dwindled, and indeed for many years in the Dark Ages the city was abandoned. It only revived in the twelfth century when the Counts of Provence, and later the Aragon and Angevin counts, made Aix their capital. The exiled King of Naples, also Duke of Anjou and Count of Provence, one René (called by his subjects Good King René, because of his benevolence and culture) brought Aix to fame in the period 1442–80 – the golden age of Provence. He introduced the silkworm, the muscatel grape, restored the courtly games of chivalry and encouraged painters, writers, musicians and troubadours. The university had been founded in 1413, and Aix has ever since been regarded as a cultured, civilised centre of the Arts. Not even the barbarous wars of religion, nor equally barbarous *citoyens* of the French Revolutions could diminish this fine reputation. In the seventeenth- and eighteenth centuries, the great mansions or *hôtels*, elegant streets, squares and fountains were built by the Provençal nobility, prelates, judges and counsellors.

The revolutionary leader, the Marquis de Mirabeau, an ugly, wicked, scandalous, impoverished and brilliant rascal, was elected to the States General in 1789 and sat for Aix as MP. The most elegant boulevard outside Paris, although a mere 500 metres, was named after him. The Cours Mirabeau, with four rows of large plane trees, has on its north side cafés, restaurants, book and antique shops and is faced on the south side by smart seventeenth and eighteenth-century mansions (look at Nos. 4, 10, 14, 16,19, 20 and 38). Aix has more than 160 elegant *hôtels* and anyone with architectural leanings should visit Rue de l'Opéra (Nos. 18, 24 and 26); Rue Mazarin (Nos. 10, 12 and 14); Rue 4 Septembre (Nos. 9, 11 and 18); Rue Emeric David (Nos. 16, 18, 22, 25 and 26) and Rue Gaston de Saporta (Nos. 10, 17, 19, 21 and 23). The Pavilion de Vendôme, built in 1667, at 34 Rue Célony is perhaps the best known town mansion.

Marseille, only 29 km away (a sort of big brother), has developed at the expense of Aix which, with a population of 126,000, is now a mere sub-prefecture town. Nevertheless, Aix is indisputably a university town with natural style and grace, and maintains its fine reputation. Appropriately, it is twinned with our town of Bath. Tobias Smollett, visiting in the eighteenth century to take the waters, admitted many of its inhabitants 'are persons of fashion, they are well bred, gay and sociable'.

Places to see

The Office Municipal du Tourisme is at No. 2, Place du Général de Gaulle, tel. 42-26-02-93, which is at the west end of the Cours Mirabeau. It is also close to the Casino Municipal, Bd de la République, tel. 42-26-30-33 and ten minutes' walk from the eighteenth-century thermal baths at 55 Cours Sextius, tel. 42-26-00-42. The old town is a rectangle with the

Cours Mirabeau as its southern base. Locate the Rue Clemenceau which leads into the Place St Honoré, the Rue des Bagniers, the Rue Mejanes, the Place de l'Hôtel de Ville, and the Rue Espariat (look at No. 10). Keep walking gently north towards the cathedral and cloisters of St Sauveur (which has a fifth-century baptistry and a famous triptych of the Burning Bush by Nicholas Froment, court painter to King René). Nearby is the Tapestry Museum (18 Beauvais tapestries) in the old Archbishop's Palace. On your way back, call in at the Museum of old Aix (*santons*, puppets and dolls), at 17 Rue Gaston de Saporta, and then the Clock Tower, courtyard and Mejanes library (300,000 old tomes) in the Hôtel de Ville. There are fountains in most of the little squares and four large ones in the Cours Mirabeau (Grande, Neufs-Canons, Eau Chaude and Roi René).

There are two more significant museums to see. The Granet Fine Arts and Archeology (closed Tuesday) is in a seventeenth-century priory in the Quartier Mazarin, SE of the east end of the Cours Mirabeau. Fran,cois Granet, a friend of Ingres (see his *Jupiter* and *Thetis*) contributed 500 pieces to this fine collection. The Provençal works are from Van Loo, Emile Loubon, Le Nain, Pierre Puget and Guillemot. The French schools of the Renaissance of Fontainebleau are well represented. Paul Cézanne, the most celebrated Aix painter, has eight minor works. There are two other fine collections of the Proven,cal *faience* (ceramics from Moustiers, Apt, Avignon and Marseille) and the most ancient collection of Gaulish sculptures mainly excavated from the site at Egremont, 2½ km north of the town.

The little Musée Paul Arbaud, at 2a Rue du 4 Septembre (closed Sundays), lies between the Granet and the Cours Mirabeau, and contains a collection of Provençal art, local ceramics, sculpture and a fine library. Look for the seventeenth-century Fontaine des Quatre Dauphins (actually dolphins) on the way.

It is worth making a little pilgrimage north beyond the cathedral to see the Paul Cézanne studio at No. 9 Ave. Paul Cézanne (closed Tuesdays), tel. 42-21-06-53. An unappreciated native of Aix, he spent much of his life in Paris. He also lived at 23 Rue Boulegon in old Aix and walked to work to his *atelier*. On his death in 1906 the studio, left exactly as it was then, has become an artistic pilgrimage. Sadly most of his famous, and now very expensive, paintings are scattered around the world's rich museums.

Touring

On the outskirts of Aix are two very diverse sights. In the suburbs 4 km due west at 1 Ave. Marcel Pagnon is the large Vasarely Foundation Museum (linked with that in Gordes) of the ultra-modern works of the brilliant and exotic Hungarian artist of that name. However, his twentieth-century geometric style may not be everybody's cup of tea. The aluminium building is situated on the Jas de Bouffan hillside (closed Tuesdays).

By contrast, the excavations of the Ligurian tribe's oppidum at Egremont, north for 2½ km on the D14 (closed Tuesday), has produced a wealth of information. Ramparts, gateway, round towers and houses have been excavated, dating from the second or third century BC. The finds are in the Granet Museum.

Excursions can also be made westwards to the local vineyards of Coteaux d'Aix, where there are 60 wine châteaux. (Beaulieu, Lacoste and Fonscolombe white wines have all won international medals.) There are also no less then 17 co-ops, including Venelles on the N96, and Mont Ste Victoire (at Puyloubier). The wines of Palette, a small A.O.C., are to be found 5 km SE. The Tourist Office has daily guided tours at 10 a.m. and 3.30 p.m. and out of season on Wednesday (English) and Saturday (French) afternoons starting at 3 p.m. They are quite expensive at 40 francs but good value nonetheless.

Food and drink in Aix

One speciality of Aix is a sweet marzipan biscuit called a *calisson*. The almond production of Aix is the greatest in Europe. Try them on the Cours Mirabeau at the shops, Bremond at No. 36 and Bechard at No. 12. The sixteenth-century Provençal poet Claude Brueys wrote *De tartos e de*

calissons, E de touto autro counfituro and the English visitors
on the Grand Tour guzzled *calissons* on their visit to Aix.
Local chocolates are to be found at La Reine Jeanne at
No. 32.

One of the best open air food markets are held in the Place
des Precheurs on Tuesday, Thursday and Saturday mornings,
also in the Place de la Madeleine and Place de Verdun.

The major event in the year is the summer music festival,
which has been held for three weeks in July for over 40 con-
secutive years. Operas and concerts are given in the Théâtre
de l'Archeveché, or cathedral or cloisters of St Sauveur, tel.
42-23-37-81. Hotel reservations can also be made at the
same time, on the same number.

The best hotels in Aix are the Cézanne, 40 Ave. Victor-
Hugo and Le Pigonnet, Ave. du Pigonnet. The best value
budget hotels are des Quatre Dauphins, 54 Rue Roux
Alpheron, tel. 42-38-16-39 (being renovated); the Sully, 69
Bd Carnot, tel. 42-38-11-77 (run by two little old ladies who
play the piano); the Pax, 29 Rue Espariot, tel. 42-76-24-79;
and Vendôme, 10 Cours des Minîmes, tel. 42-64-45-01.

One can certainly eat well in Aix. We counted 16 different
kinds of olives (16–22 francs per kilo) in the Place Precheurs
market and *tapenade* (olive oil paste with herbs, capers and
garlic) features on many menus. La Belle Epoque café on the
Cours Mirabeau is *the* place to have your pre-lunch or pre-
dinner aperitif. After that try La Grange in Carriero de
Nazaret, La Grille, 18 Rue Portalis, or Le Terminus on Cours
Mirabeau *(pâté de sanglier, brochette à la provençale)*.

Afterwards, look in at a café-theatre or one of the many jazz
clubs. Aix has been likened to Florence, Vicenza or Rome –
indisputably the most elegant town in Provence.

CHAPTER THIRTEEN: MARSEILLE

Greek Phocean traders from Marseille, Pytheas amongst them, sailed to the British Isles, Cornwall and Devon in particular, bartering wines for cargoes of tin. That was nearly 2,500 years ago!

Local history

The Greeks made the city prosperous as Massilia and the Romans happily took over a wealthy trading town on their arrival in 271 BC as allies against Carthage. The Roman general Marius protected Marseille against the Teutons and Ambrons in three years of savage fighting from 125–122 BC. But the town backed Pompey (the loser) in 49 BC and the winner, Julius Caesar, took his revenge. He disbanded their fleet and gave preference to Arles and Narbonne. Marseille stagnated until the eleventh century when it became a Crusader port (along with Aigues-Mortes).

The town was evangelised by a Roman officer called Victor who was horribly put to death in 228 AD – and later canonised. A later abbot-saint, John Cassien, founded an abbey in 410 AD above a cave in which Victor and other Christian martyrs were buried. Today the fortified St Victor Basilica still stands proudly on the south side of the old harbour. Many relics from the Holy Land are to be seen there – St Andrew's Cross, hairs from St Paul's beard, one of St Peter's teeth, one of St Anthony's fingers, one of Lazarus' ribs and St Cassien's head – despite sacking by the Saracens in 923 AD. The Black Death decimated the population in 1339, and the town was pillaged by the Aragon fleet in 1423.

Fortunately King René recognised its importance. He fortified the town, built the tower of St Jean and imported Italian troubadours to sing their romantic songs.

Along with the rest of Provence, Marseille was absorbed by the Kingdom of France in 1481 AD and King François I built two key forts — Notre-Dame-de-la-Garde and another on the small island of If (made famous by Dumas' Count of Monte Cristo). During the wars of religion most of Provence were Protestant supporters but Marseille remained Catholic.

As Marseilles has always been one of the chief commercial towns of France it comes as no surprise to learn that in 1599 AD the King encouraged the formation of the first Chamber of Commerce of all France. But the Sun King, Louis XIV, ordered the destruction of the ramparts (along with scores of other French cities) but also authorised the city to be increased in size. Later Minister Colbert gave the town a trading monopoly with the Levant.

The French Revolution

Marseille became one of the first cities in France to embrace the revolutionary ideals in 1789. Their workers, 'batallion of 10 August', adopted the northern battle song, which became known as the *Marseillaise*. Now it is probably the best known song/tune in the world. Ironically enough in 1793/4, taking sides with the Girondins party, the inhabitants became victims of the White Terror inflicted by Barras and Fréron who declared the city *'ville sans nom'*. They put hundreds of *citoyens* to death (the guillotine was sited in the Canebière) and ordered a port blockade which reduced the number of merchant ships arriving each year from 3,000 to less than 100. The English sea blockade ensured privation. No wonder the restoration of the old monarchy in 1814 (restored by perfidious Albion) was welcomed. The acquisition of Algeria across the Mediterranean pond in 1830, and the opening of the Suez Canal, brought great wealth to the town. In the Second World War the Wehrmacht destroyed the old town on the north side of the old harbour, since it was too easy for the members of the Resistance to hide in the narrow backstreets. Oil and gas refineries at the nearby Fos-sur-Mer and Etang de Berre have made the Marseille port complex the most important in France.

Modern Marseille

With a population of just under a million, Marseille is the capital of Provence. This huge modern city gives little impression of being interested in the past and Le Corbusier's Cité Radieuse, built in 1952 (off the Bd. Michelet), is still quite shocking to the senses — quite a contrast to the stately Basilica of Notre-Dame-de-la-Garde, known as Bonne Mère, overlooking the old port. A pilgrimage takes place there on 15 August each year.

So, treat Marseille as a large, modern city with some areas to be visited with caution, particularly between the main station and the Canebière. There are twelve museums, of which the Maritime, Roman Docks, Cantini and Fine Arts are the most interesting, although the Borely Château houses two museums and the Grobet-Labadie (Provençal armour, sculptures and tapestries) are certainly worth a visit. The Museum of Old Marseille is housed in the exquisite Maison Diamentée. Besides the Opéra there are no less than 17 theatres and 10 cinemas. The Tourist Office, No. 4, La Canebière, tel. 91-54-91-11, publishes a monthly booklet entitled *Nouvelles de Marseille*, crammed full of entertainment news. On our last visit Verdi's *Don Carlos* was being performed at the Opéra, a Marcel Proust play at the Théâtre de la Criée, Kafka at the Théâtre Off, Feydeau at the Galas-Karsenly-Herbert and a concert of Provençal music was performed at the Centre Culturel Provençal du Roudelet-Felibren.

The main sights are the Old Port where a score of restaurants or brasseries will tempt you to a glass of anis or pastis, or a meal of *bouillabaisse*; the two cathedrals; the Church of St Laurent; the two forts; and the Canebière which ends at the Old Port (near the Tourist Office). However, there are seven parks in which to stroll and picnic, Jardin du Pharo, Parc Borely and Jardin Colline Puget being the most attractive. Rather surprisingly there are no less than six beaches between the Pharo (lighthouse) and the southern Plages du Prado.

The markets of Marseille are a colourful feature. There are five food markets, two fish markets and six morning flower markets. The garlic market *(aux aulx)* is worth seeking out for the aromatic pink and purple bulbs. The ferry boat service plies between the Mairie and the Place aux Huiles. The Métro with 23 stations is the quickest way around town. The larger boats leave from the Quai des Belges, tel. 91-55-50-09, or try S.N.C.M., 61 Bd. des Dames for the photogenic Château d'If and the larger Ile du Friol. During summer there are boat tours (highly recommended) to the deep-water *calanques* along the coast. Coach tours of the town leave every day (except on Sunday) at 1O a.m. from June to September from outside the Tourist Office. The itinerary is the Porte d'Aix, cathedral, St Laurent church, Town Hall, Notre-Dame-de-la-Garde, Corniche President-Kennedy, Parc Borely, Le Corbusier township and back down La Canebière. Don't drive in Marseille (and parking is difficult): visit on foot, use the Métro or take the bus tour of the town. The two best views for photographers are from the Parc de Pharo and from Notre-Dame-de-la-Garde.

The main events of the year are: the summer festival of theatre, opera and concerts in July and August: the Santon Fair (the religious crib clay figures and costumes) from November to 6 January; and on 2 February the Candlemas Festival in the abbey of St Victor. In spring the port is host to an international sailing week and in October the Phocea cup is held, a race for fifty vintage sailing boats.

Keen walkers should get in touch with the Société des Excursionistes Marsaillais (through the Tourist Office) for tours by foot cross-country to the impressive *calanques* at En Vau, Morgiou and Sormiou. These deep blue creeks are ringed on three sides with red rocks, often with a small sandy beach and can only be reached by boat.

Hotels and restaurants

Marseille has over 150 hotels. I have chosen a few modest ones in the centre of town which are probably noisy but safe!

The Azur, 24 Cours Fr. Roosevelt, tel. 91-42-74-38; the Princess, 16 Rue des Feuillants, tel. 91-54-15-61; La Bourse, 4 Rue Paradis, tel. 91-33-74-75; and Pavillon, 27 Rue Pavillon, tel. 91-33-76-90. They are all quite close together, near a Métro station and official car park. The Gambetta, 49 Allées Leon-Gambetta, tel. 91-62-07-88, has street parking outside the hotel.

Around the Cours Julien you will find many good budget restaurants including Le Tire Bouchon, Le Caucase, Dar Djerba, Facéties, La Garbure and Chez Benoit. You will find all of them have local fish dishes, some typical Provençal dishes and, of course, North African couscous on the Quai de Rive Neuve. Opposite, on the Quai de Port, all restaurants serve *bouillabaisse* (fish stew cooked with saffron, dorade and crab) or *oursinade*, a soup of sea urchins, crab and oysters).

CHAPTER FOURTEEN:
PROVENCE-ON-SEA

Nobody goes to Provence for sea bathing — or do they? Along the Mediterranean coast of the Bouche-du-Rhône (not the French Riviera to the east) are 282 km of coastline, plus another 30–40 km in the Gard and an unbelievable 350 sand or pebble beaches, coves, bays and creeks *(calanques)*. Many of them can only be approached by boat from the sea side. On my last visit to Marseille I queried this fact with the departmental Tourist Office who confirmed it!

Recommended beaches

This chapter identifies some of the better beaches journeying from west to east, i.e. part of the Gard to La Ciotat. Le Grau du Roi and Port-Camargue south of Aigues-Mortes are fishing villages that have gone up-market, with a marina and excellent beaches. Heading east towards Stes Maries-de-la-Mer are 30 km of good sandy beaches. Along the narrow spit of the Golfe de Beauluc past the Pointe de Beauluc, the lighthouses of Beauluc and Faraman, one comes to the Plage de Piemenson. This is south of the large Salin de Giraud salt-marshes just west of the entrance to the Grand Rhône River.

Just off the N568 are two more beaches — Plage de Fos and Plage Port-de-Bouc (but mind the oil tankers). Inland around the large Etang de Berre are many more beaches, Ranquet-Plage, Istres, St Chamas, Berre and a long spit off Vitrolles and Marignane called Plage de Jai. SW of Martigues on the peninsula of the Estaque are more civilised beaches, des Laurons, and many small coves off the D9 including Sausset-les-Pins and Rouet-Plage. These two villages have a distinct Riviera flavour about them — smart villas, exotic vegetation and trees, and good restaurants.

In Sausset-les-Pins try La Reserve, tel. 42-45-06-04 or, in Carry-le-Rouet, La Tuiliere, Ave. Draio-de-la-Mer, tel. 42-45-02-96 and Le Carry, Bd. Jourde, tel. 42-45-02-90.

Marseille itself has five beaches on its south side, called *Catalans sable*, *Bains militaires*, *Prophète sable*, *Carlton rochers* and two Plages du Prado. Try dropping anchor in the Frioul Islands maritime park (250 hectares) close to the Château d'If and exploring the islands of Ratonneau and Pomegues.

For good swimmers, the *calanques* provide superb bathing and underwater exploration, but you need a boat or yacht to get there. Off the Massif du Puget (and good walkers could use the Grande Randonnée 98) are a score of *calanques* called Callelonque, La Mounine, Marseilleveyre, Podestat, Sormiou, Morgiou, Sugiton, L'Oule, En-Vau, Port-Pin and Port-Miou until one reaches the smart, Riviera-like resort town of Cassis.

For nudists there is Bonnieu beach near Martigues, the 'Arles' beach/Piemanson near Salin de Giraud, and Sugiton *calanque* beach (a one-hour walk from the car park on Mont Luminy).

Cassis

Cassis (pop. 6,500) has four beaches of shingle-sand (Bestouan, L'Arène, Le Courton and La Grande Mer) and is enchanting with white villas, winding streets, exotic flowers and 200 hectares of vines growing on the slopes producing dry, golden white wines. The four modest hotels are the Auberge du Joli Bois, Route de la Gineste, tel. 42-01-02-68; Le Commerce, 2 Rue St-Claire, tel. 42-01-09-10; Le Provençal, 7 Ave. Victor-Hugo, tel. 42-01-72-13; and Auberge Maguy, Ave. du Revestel, tel. 42-01-72-21. The Tourist Office in Place P. Baragnon, tel. 42-01-71-17, organises excursions and boat rentals. The town museum is free but the municipal casino may cost a little more!

La Ciotat

Follow the coast SE past Cap Canaille, preferably by the Corniche des Crètes, round the Cap d'Aigle to the large town of La Ciotat. This fourth-century BC Greek settlement is now a town of 32,000 people and a curious mixture of shipbuilding (employing 6,000), a large marina and tourism. The new man-made beaches to the east, as well as La Ciotat-Plage on the north of the harbour, offer several choices for bathers. The large dockyards are on the west side of the large bay and beyond are the *calanques* of Muguel and Figuerolles, with the formidable Cap d'Aigle in between and the Ile Verte 2 km out to sea. La Ciotat has not quite the same charm as Cassis, but it does have an attractive old port, several seventeenth-century chapels, *calanques* and beaches! Modest hotels include Beaurivage, 1 Bd. Beaurivage, tel. 42-83-09-68; Bellevue, 3 Bd. Guerin, tel. 42-71-86-01; La Marine, 1 Ave. Fernard-Gassion, tel. 42-08-35-11; and Plaisance, 15 Ave. Fernand-Gassion, tel. 42-08-35-11; and Plaisance, 15 Ave. Franklin-Roosevelt, tel. 42-83-10-19. The last two have good-value restaurants.

Boats can be hired from Jany Nautic, 3 Bd. A.-France, and Bateau le Voltigeur, 11 Quai Général de Gaulle have a regular ferry boat service to the Ile Verte, tel. 42-83-11-44.

CHAPTER FIFTEEN:
THE CAMARGUE

The huge flat triangular area of the River Rhône valley, known as La Camargue, was declared in 1970 to be a National Park. Nearly 800 square km, of which 70 per cent is marshland, extend from Aigues-Mortes to the west (the Canal du Rhône and Le Petit Rhône) to Salin-de-Badon and Salin-de-Giraud on the banks of the Grand Rhône in the east — a distance of 50 km. Arles and St Gilles are the two northern corners of the Bouches-du-Rhône triangle. Excluding the three towns mentioned, the so-called capital of the region is the curious town of Stes Maries-de-la-Mer on the coast (pop. 2,000). Once there were three fine churches — the salt abbeys of Psalmody, Sylvereal and Ulmet. The coastline is in constant conflict with the elements as 20 million cubic metres of mud, sand and gravel are swept down the River Rhône each year and the salty Mediterranean fights back with regular fierce storms. But the retained silt has lifted the height of the delta by 10 metres in 2,000 years!

The hinterlands of the Camargue

The northern areas of the Camargue, known as the hinterlands, are now cultivated with rice (4,000 hectares) which helps the constant desalination process, plus some vines producing *vin de sable* (they grow amazingly well in sandy, salty soil), maize and rape crops and some fruit trees. Other trees are still quite rare, but poplars, tamarisks and willows can be seen as well as the ubiquitous bamboo clumps which act as wind breaks. The salt-marsh area has been worked since the thirteenth-century, particularly around Salin-de-Giraud and Aigues-Mortes, and 600,000 tonnes of salt are produced each year. Between March and September the paddy fields are flooded one foot deep with salt water, and by the end of the hot summer evaporation has left salt crystals which are piled up into huge white glittering piles called *camelles*, up to 20 metres high. Our first glimpse of these strange man-made hills was south of the road N113 between Salon-de-Provence and Arles. This is the desert-like area know as the Crau Plain.

The southern Camargue

The main traditional Camargue in the southern delta of marshes, sand, little canals, the occasional farm *(mas)*, with protective sand dunes and bamboo windbreaks, is famous throughout the world for its melancholy charm. About 30 ranches or *mas* (some of them ranch-hotels) breed 5,000 dangerous little black bulls (*manades*) which appear in the bull rings all over southern France. The fights are known as *cocardes*, since around their necks the bulls carry a rosette which is a target for seizure by the bullfighter, who is called a *rasetteur*. The *courses provençales* are very popular, and take place in many villages in the streets and in the arenas. The *gardiens*, or Camargue cowboys, who live in white-washed cottages called *cabines* ride and train the equally famous white horses (born brown but becoming white after three or four years). The *gardiens'* riding skill is tested at the *ferrades* when the yearling bull-steers are caught and branded. The men are equipped with long tridents called *ficherouns* to keep the bulls at a relatively safe distance! These French cowboys date from 1572, and their traditions are nurtured by the Confrérie des Gardiens. The bulls' lineage dates from early Roman times and the horses are thought to be similar to the prehistoric beasts slaughtered at Solutré in Burgundy.

The Camargue National Reserve

This covers 14,000 hectares of the region around the south of the large Etang de Vaccares. The most famous of the 400 bird species are the pink flamingos, which can be seen in summer. In full flight they are a majestic sight. Bird migrants *(les passereaux)* come and go — duck and teal, heron and cranes, and many more which can be seen in the 12-hectare Ornithological Park of Pont-de-Gau, tel. 90-47-82-62, on the D570 just north of Stes Maries-de-la-Mer. In the Orni Park, where you have three choices of walks (short, medium and long), we saw storks nesting, honey buzzards, black kites, marsh harriers, Egyptian vultures, buzzards, herring gulls, greenshanks, grey herons and cormorants. Unfortunately we failed to see the kingfishers, great reed warblers, moustached warblers or golden oriels! The fortunate or skilled watcher can see boar, foxes, weasels, beavers, badgers, tree-frogs, ter-rapins, water snakes and a variety of eels in the lagoons. Since 1928 all flora and fauna have been protected and the vege-tation and flowers on the Rieges Islands in the reserve are spectacular.

The best time to see the Camargue is in the late spring or autumn. The crowds in summer (and the mosquitos at night) come to ride the white horses in the marshes or on the beach (at about 50 francs per hour accompanied by a *gardien*). Alternatively, jeep tours are on offer, or better still a 75-minute boat trip up the Petit Rhône (3 km west of Stes Maries-de-la-Mer or vice versa from Arles), tel. 90-97-81-68.

In the Grand Tour (see Chapter 2), I have mentioned the route we usually take from the east or the west, but of course Arles or St Gilles are the best bases, with the roads D570 and D179 respectively feeding SW or SE into the Camargue. Out of season the minor roads linking Plage de Piemenson, Salin-de-Giraud, Salin-de-Badon, Villeneuve, Méjanes (amusement centre ideal for children, mock bullfights, pony trekking, elec-tric railway and horsedrawn carriages) and Albaron (with a thirteenth-century tower) are free of traffic. But the D570 from Arles to Les Stes Maries is always busy.

Les Stes Maries

Now I must admit that apart from the legendary fortified church (black and gloomy) with its shrine, crypt, relics and chapels, we found little of interest in Les Stes Maries. It is a garish tourist trap with a new boat marina, busy fishing port and swarming with very importunate and grasping gypsies who beg frankly and aggressively before driving off in their cars to have lunch back at the *mas*. For those with stamina the town in season has non-stop entertainment, but watch your wallets and remember to say *'Merci, NON'*.

Excursions can be made by *mini-croisière*, a splendid, old-fashioned paddleboat called Le Tiki III, which chugs gently round the canals of the Camargue. The boat takes (just) 200 passengers, costs about 50 francs per head and takes 1¼ hours, tel. 90-97-81-68. The embarkation point is 2½ km west of the town centre (40 minutes' walk along the coast road) from 20 March to 14 November. The ranch Le Gitan at Port Camargue, tel. 66-5l-99-42, will take you on Land Rover safari cruises around the Camargue. Safari Photo du Delta, 8 Ave. de la République, Place des Gitans, tel. 90-47-89-33, offer you a photographic tour of the Camargue, bird, bull and white horse spotting and guaranteed pink flamingos.

Orvac, Place des Marseillaises, Marseille, tel. 91-50-33-45, offer two-day ecological tours of the Camargue from 410-650 francs including accommodation and transport. They also offer a four-day tour the weekend of 1 May from 710 francs for the Fête des Gardiens in Arles, attending the festival, followed by a day of sightseeing in the Camargue. Every Sunday from April to September there are bull-running rosette races (*cocardes*). On 24–25 May is the celebrated Gypsy Pilgrimage with a procession of their patron saint Sarah into the sea, which is repeated on the Sunday closest to 22 October. In mid-June is the *Fête de la Maintenance* with rodeos and bull races. On the third Sunday in July are the Fêtes Virginienco and 14–17 August is the Feria Saintoise. There are costumed festivals, *farandoles, abrivados*, bull branding, horse races and bull shows. The Romany nomads and travelling folk assemble from all over Europe and carry Sarah's statue, with bands playing and flowers thrown, from the church to the sea. In the evening the *romaniche* parade the streets – swarthy, passionate and probably romantic men and women dressed in their exotic finery.

There are also 25 km of beaches and sand dunes to explore

99

(including a nudist beach 3 km away). They are regarded as the poor man's Riviera, but one can windsurf, sail, and explore the area on bicycle or horse, even on foot. Modest hotels include the Mediterranean, 4 Bd. F. Mistral, tel. 90-97-82-09 or de la Plage, Ave. de la République, tel. 90-97-84-77. There are dozens of small restaurants offering meals at 50–75 francs, including the Lou Penequet on the seafront.

Key information points

- Camargue Information Centre at Gînes, 5 km north on N570 of Les-Stes-Maries, tel. 90-97-86-32.
- Camargue National Reserve – information centre at La Capellière on D36A north of Salin-de-Badon on east side of Vaccarès lagoon.
- Musée Camarguais, also on N570, at Pont de Rousty, 20 km north of Les Stes Maries, tel. 90-97-10-82.
- Musée du Boumian (typical Camargue life) just north of Les Stes Maries and south of Gînes (closed Tuesday).
- Méjanes Amusement Centre, tel. 90-97-10-10, has a wide range of entertainments.
- The Baroncelli Museum in old Hôtel de Ville in Les Stes Maries (closed Wednesday) houses a complete Camargue collection (books and birds, paintings and furniture and cowboy lifestyle).
- The Tourist Office is in the Ave. Van-Gogh, tel. 90-07-82-55.

Aigues-Mortes

Technically speaking, Aigues-Mortes (pop. 4,500) in the Gard department is probably just outside the Camargue. The city of the 'dead waters' is a perfect example of a medieval fortified walled town lying rather forlornly in the remote flat, salty marshlands. The moat is filled in but the city *donjon*, 30 metres high, called the Tour de Constance, still keeps a watch for the returning crusaders of King St Louis in 1248. Laid out on a grid pattern similar to the bastides of Aquitaine, the town has five gates defended by twin watch towers (two with portcullis and machicoulis). The walk all round the ramparts (l½ km) takes three quarters of an hour. The silting up of the river saved the town from destruction by marauding barbarians and was later used as a prison for the Huguenots in the eleventh and twelfth centuries. Now it is dependent on income from the 250,000 tonnes of salt produced locally. The Tourist Office is in Place St-Louis, tel. 66-51-92-00. The Hôtel l'Escale, Ave. Tour de Constance, tel. 66-51-92-10, is inexpensive.

If you are visiting the Camargue please make a small detour to see this classic little *Carcassonne*. Excursions can be made to Le Grau du Roi, an up-and-coming seaside resort with long sandy beaches that is still an attractive fishing village. Teillan castle is 13 km WNW and Les Salins-du-Midi are salt mines which can be visited during July and August.

CHAPTER SIXTEEN:
ARLES

It is difficult to realise that twentieth-century Arles, on the eastern banks of the River Rhône, 40 km from the Mediterranean, and on the crossroads of Hannibal's march from Spain to Italy, now has a population half that of two thousand years ago. The ancient Roman seaport of Arles (Arelate), the capital of Gaul, near the many salt lagoons, then had a population of 100,000.

Roman Arles

In 49 BC, Julius Caesar founded here a colony for his sixth legion: a town with ramparts, tower and gates, a water and sewage system with public baths and lavatories of white marble. There was a Roman imperial mint, a trading centre for arms, gold and silver *objets d'art*, textiles and glass works. Its wines and olive oil were as famous then as now. But earlier still, in 104 BC, Marius, the Roman pro-consul of Massilia (Marseille), had built a canal linking Arles with the Gulf of Fos so that the Roman trading ships could enter the Rhône river valley. The poet Ausonius described the prosperous town as 'Gallula Roma', the little gallic Rome on the junction of the Agrippan Way leading north to Lyon and the Aurelian Way leading west and east. The Romans bred bulls in the Camargue — small, nippy, black and dangerous — to fight in the arenas of Arles, Orange and Nîmes. Constantine the Great built a palace here in about 314 AD and Emperor Honorius made Arles the capital of the three Gauls (France, Spain *and* Britain!).

At the decline of the Roman Empire the Visigoths occupied Arles from 480–536, followed by the Franks and the Saracens who came in 730. It became a kingdom between 839 and 1032, a Crusader port and part of the Holy Roman Empire. The Kingdom of Arles included Burgundy and most of Provence, and in 1482 was incorporated into the Kingdom of France (some thirty years after the English were defeated in Aquitaine to the west). Then for 600 years Arles' importance gradually declined in favour of Aix, Avignon, Nîmes and, of course, Marseille. River traffic became obsolete when the railway arrived in the 1870s.

Modern Arles

After the Second World War the population had decreased to 20,000 but has since steadily increased to 50,000 in line with prosperity for the whole of the region of Provence. The salt and rice crops of the Camargue and the Crau and, of course, tourism are important.

Arles still has numerous roads feeding into it: the N570 from Avignon and the north; the N453 and N113 from the east (Salon and Marseille); from the south comes the D35 parallel to the canal to the Port de Fos; and from the triangle of the Camargue the D570 and D36. Finally from the west, lies the N113 (Nîmes), and the N572 from St Gilles.

The Tourist Office, opposite the Jardin d'Eté in the Esplanade Charles de Gaulle, tel. 90-96-29-35, produces a town plan linking the ten major *antiquities*. A ticket costing 35 francs will enable you to visit *all* of them, including the museums.

Places to see

The Roman amphitheatre was built by the same architect as that of Nîmes and could seat over 25,000 spectators. In the Middle Ages 200 houses and a church were built within the amphitheatre, using the high walls as protective town ramparts, but in 1825 they were excavated and now many bullfights, plays and concerts take place in the arena. Three of the original four towers are still in place.

A short walk away is the Roman theatre, which was built in 1 BC and drew audiences of 7,000 spectators. You need a lot of imagination to recreate Emperor Augustus' artistry but there are several clues: two marble columns, a curtain trench, twenty rows of seating and the orchestra site. The famous Venus of Arles was discovered here in 1651 and is now in the Louvre. In July there is the annual drama festival within the walled garden.

The fourth-century Baths of Constantine are near the banks of the Rhône, once part of an imperial palace. The ancient Roman burial grounds, the melancholy Alyscamps, lined with poplars amongst the sarcophagi, lie alongside the little Canal de Craponne; the burial ground and chapel are eight minutes' walk SE of the Tourist Office. The old Roman forum is now the Place du Forum with plane trees and Van Gogh's Café du Soir.

Besides its Roman legacies, Arles has been a painters' paradise. Van Gogh painted here *L'Arlesienne, Starry Night, Alyscamps, Sunflowers* and a famous self-portrait. More recently Picasso, who loved Arles, donated a collection of drawings which are on display in Musée Réattu.

The main Romanesque church of St Trophime, dedicated to a Greek apostle, is near the Roman theatre. St Augustine was consecrated first bishop of England here in 597 AD by St Virgil, Bishop of Arles and Frederick Barbarossa was crowned King of Arles here in 1178. The twelfth-century Portal on the west front, and particularly the cloisters, should be seen.

Arles is rich in museums. My favourite is the Arlaten (closed Mondays out of season), inspired by Frédéric Mistral. If you really want to know how the provincial Provençaux lived, what they wore, ate, drank and their crafts and legends, then the Arlaten will inform, amuse and interest. The Réattu on the river banks in the fifteenth-century Priory of the Knights of St John of Jerusalem belonged to the painter Jacques Réattu (1760–1833) and, naturally, three galleries exhibit his work. Besides Picasso's 57 drawings, look at Henri Rousseau's paintings of the Camargue and the eighteenth-century Provençal school. Altogether this is a surprisingly well balanced collection (Gaugin, Dufy, Utrillo and Leger) including tapestries, sculptures and a modern photography exhibition on the second floor.

The Museums of Pagan Art and Christian Art are near the seventeenth-century Town Hall and the Arlaten. The former is in the church of St Anne and the latter in the old Jesuit College. Both rank amongst the great lapidary museums of Europe.

Arles is a small compact town, and all the main sights can easily be visited on foot. There are many reasons for the visitor to stop, ponder and wonder. For example, there are the Roman antiquities, the excellent museums, tracing Van Gogh's meteoric painting career (Café du Soir, Café de Nuit, the Yellow House, the Bridge and other clues – some have vanished, some still exist), and the unique Musée Arlaten (its thirty rooms really warrant two visits), but it is also worth remembering that Arles had two unique historical links with Britain. The Romans made Arles capital of *our* island, and our first bishop of England came from the same town!

Local festivals

As capital of the Camargue, a fête of the *gardiens* (cowboys looking after the 5,000 Camargue fighting bulls and the wild horses) is held in Arles on the last Sunday in April. The main bullfight festival is held for four days over Easter in the Arena. In July the Roman Theatre hosts an international festival of dance, music and drama and for four weeks over Christmas and the New Year a Trade Fair of *santons* is held in Arles. These semi-religious pottery figurines in authentic dress are a feature of Provence. One local artisan is Ferriol, 2 bis, Chemin de Barrol.

Hotels and restaurants

Arles has plenty of hotels and restaurants. The best is the Jules César on the Bd. des Lices in a seventeenth-century monastery. Budget hotels with easy parking are at the north end of town, through the ramparts in the Place Lamartine, beside the River Rhône. We have stayed at the Hôtel Terminus and Van Gogh, No. 1-3, tel. 90-96-12-32, and next door No. 5 at the Hôtel de France, tel. 90-96-01-24. Three more are in the Place Voltaire, three minutes' walk into town through the ramparts from the Place Lamartine. The Voltaire at No. 1, tel. 90-96-13-58; Le Rhône at No. 11, tel. 90-96-43-70; and the Gauguin at No. 5, tel. 90-96-14-35. Good-value restaurants include the Hostellerie des Arènes, 62 Rue du Refuge opposite the arena (try *Carré d'agneau provençale*); the Magali in Rue Chavary which has a 50-franc menu including *pâté de campagne camarguais, daube provençale* or *filet de merlu blanc*. Le Galoubet, 18 Rue du Dr-Fanton (near Place du Forum) has *poulet sauce provençale, courgettes la ratatouille*. The Lou Gardian, 70 Rue 4 Septembre, has *cuisses de grenouille provençales* (frogs' legs).

A local speciality is *fougasse*, a pretzel-shaped bread with bits of ham baked in it. On Wednesday mornings visit the open air market along Bd. Emile Combes, and on Saturday mornings go to the one on the Bd. des Lices, the main road running west-east opposite the Jardin d'Hiver and the Post Office. The colourful wooden tourist train (ideal for children) wends its way around town, starting outside the Tourist Office. There are tourist boat tours linking with Avignon. They leave from the Quai Lamartine, next to the Place Lamartine. The best cafés for watching the world go by are in the Place du Forum or on the Bd. des Lices.

Touring

Arles is an ideal base for exploring Provence. Equidistant from Nîmes, Avignon, Salon and Les Stes Maries-de-la-Mer, as well as Tarascon, St Rémy and Les Baux. It even has a train service to Nîmes and Avignon. The Office of Tourisme arranges tours of the city, to the Camargue, a Van Gogh tour (in summer twice a week), and Montmajour Abbey and Daudet's windmill at Fontvieille are a few km up the road.

In this calm, peaceful town (calm in relation to Marseille and Avignon) it is hard to believe that Bizet wrote the music for the dazzling *L'Arlesiène* by Daudet or that Van Gogh, having achieved his painting miracles, should then cut off his ear in 1890!

CHAPTER SEVENTEEN:
LES BAUX AND ST
REMY-DE-PROVENCE

I must confess that I had never heard of the tough, arrogant Lords of Les Baux who dominated most of Provence (80 towns) and strange outposts in Sicily and Albania. They claimed they were descended from the magus King Balthazar and included the Star of Bethlehem in their coat of arms. From the eleventh century until the late fourteenth century they ruled vigorously, aggressively and often cruelly from a classic mountain citadel 20 km NE of Arles and 6 km south of St Rémy. The D27 connects both towns and it is best if you park 200 metres before you enter this strange mysterious medieval *village perché* at the Porte Mage (Magus Gate). Les Baux means the bauxite rocks and it is part of the Alpilles mountain plateau running 20 km west-east and south of St Rémy. The village is approximately 500 metres long, 200 metres wide, and about 300 metres in height.

In 1868, Alphonse Daudet called it 'A dusty pile of ruins, sharp rocks and old emblazoned palaces, crumbling, quivering in the wind like high eagles'. And two years earlier, John Addington Symonds wrote of the warlords, 'Here they lived and flourished these feudal princes, bearing for their ensign a silver comet of sixteen rays upon a field of gules — themselves a comet race, baleful to the neighbouring lowlands, blazing with lurid splendour over wide tracts of country, a burning, raging, fiery-souled swift-handed tribe . . .'

The history of Les Baux

Once this mountain fortress with its two villages (that on the summit is deserted, that below has a population of 450) comprised 6,000 inhabitants with warriors, priests, troubadours and their ladies (plus a lot of serfs). After the line died out it became a Huguenot sanctuary, until in 1632 Louis XIII razed the castle and ramparts and gave the village to the Princes of Monaco (who in theory *still* own Les Baux). Nevertheless, much intelligent renovation work has been done and a visit (on foot) is essential. The main sights are visited by a million visitors each year! So come out of season if you can.

The sights of Les Baux

The twelfth-century church of St Vincent is my favourite in Provence, where the Shepherd's Festival − a Nativity pageant − takes place on Christmas Eve. St Vincent Square has a fine view over the valley and you will enjoy the cobbled narrow streets (Rue du Trençat, Rue de l'Eglise, Grande Rue and Rue des Fours). The Porcelets house has a Museum of Contemporary Art (closed Thursday), the Manville house (the Huguenot owners), and White Penitents Chapel should also be visited before you leave the living village to climb to the Deserted Village. In the Musée Lapidaire (Tour de Brau of the fourteenth century), tickets are on sale at 15 francs for both Museums, the Ville Morte and the castle on the mountain top. On a clear day you can see for ever − the plains of the Camargue, Arles and Montmajour Abbey to the SW and the Crau to the SE.

The hotels are frankly expensive, but the Hostellerie de la Reine, Jeanne-Maussanne, tel. 90-97-32-06, is good value. The Benvengudo and Oustau de Baumanière in the valley below are superb four-star hotels with restaurants to match.

St Rémy-de-Provence

I am not recommending that you stay at Les Baux. One alternative is north in St Rémy-de-Provence, having scrutinised the two grand Roman 'Antiques' (Arch and Cenotaph) on the D5 and the Glanum Roman ruins by the side of the road. This town of 8,000 inhabitants has 18 hotels and many are quite inexpensive − La Caume, de Provence, Villa Glanum and Ville Ferte.

St Rémy is famous for a variety of reasons. Nostradamus the astrologer was born here, and Van Gogh painted dozens of gorgeous landscapes in St Rémy in the last year of this life. Frédéric Mistral (who was born 6 km NW at Maillane) spent much of his life in St Rémy and Dr Albert Schweitzer was interned here in the First World War.

Besides the Roman antiquities there are two good museums (Lapidaire in Rue de Parege and Musée des Alpilles, Pierre de Brun — both closed Tuesdays). The twelfth-century cloisters and Romanesque Chapel of St Paul de Mausole should also be seen. The festival of the Transhumance (2,000 sheep plus shepherds in the streets) takes place at the end of May.

Another alternative place to stay is in Mausanne-les-Alpilles, a village on the D17, 4 km south of Les Baux. Perhaps you could try the Hôtel les Magnonarelles, 104 Ave. de la Vallée-des-Baux, tel. 90-97-30-25.

CHAPTER EIGHTEEN:
TARASCON AND BEAUCAIRE

Twenty km north of Arles and 25 km SW of Avignon are the twin towns of Tarascon (pop. 11,000 and Beaucaire (pop. 13,000). Between them lies the mighty River Rhône. Tarascon is in the department of the Bouches-du-Rhône and Beaucaire is in the Gard. Once the west bank belonged to France (before it became the large country we know today) and the east bank to the Holy Roman Empire. Moreover, Beaucaire was part of Languedoc and Tarascon was in Provence, thus deadly rivals. For seven centuries two mighty castles have been glowering at each other across the great divide. Cardinal Richelieu ordered the destruction of most of Beaucaire Castle in 1632 *(à bas les Huguenots)*, but since Tarascon was being used as a prison at the time, it was spared.

Beaucaire

From the thirteenth century until the mid-nineteenth century, Beaucaire was famous for its great fairs, when in July several hundred thousand traders (and people who live off traders) arrived by ship or land from all over Europe to exchange goods (and buy Côtes du Rhône wines). It seems hard to believe that 800 boats were once berthed opposite today's Beaucaire casino and château! Beaucaire Castle (closed Friday) with a panorama of the river, countryside and the old town below the château, the eighteenth-century church of Notre-Dame-des-Pommiers and the two museums (Vieux Beaucaire, 27 Rue Barbes and Lapidaire, Rue de Nîmes), plus the Hôtel de Ville, are all worth looking at. The Tourist Office is at 6 Rue Hôtel de Ville (near the canal du Rhône), tel. 66-59-26-57. In mid-summer there is an annual fête to commemorate the old medieval trading fair and bullfights are held in the arena. The hotel-restaurant Robinson, Route du Pont-du-Gard, tel. 66-59-21-32 (2½ km NW on D980) is good value and has easy parking. An interesting excursion is 5 km NW to the Abbey of St Roman with guided tours (closed Thursday).

Tarascon

Now go across the bridge to Tarascon, which has a very different history. Legend has it that after landing in the Camargue at Les Stes Maries-de-la-Mer, Martha (sister of Mary Magdalene) and her servant Marcelle followed the course of the Rhône northwards and settled in the small Roman town of Jovarnica. There she found the inhabitants terrified of a destructive amphibious monster — a dragon — that devoured farmers, shepherds, children and fishermen. Where was the friendly Roman legion, one might ask? There are many versions of the end of the story. With the sign of the Cross the monster vanished/was torn to pieces by dogs/was tamed/leapt back into the river. Nevertheless, it was a miracle. St Martha's body was 'discovered' in 1187 and became a place of pilgrimage as important as that of Lourdes. Nearly three centuries later, 'good King René', who spent his life divided between Aix and Tarascon, decided that the miracle should be commemorated by an annual fête (last Sunday in June), called Fête de la Tarasque. The monster, fitted with wheels, is pushed by eight men. This green papier mâché beast, complete with prickly scales, is animated by young men lurking within!

Places to visit

The twelfth-century castle was renovated by King René and is a perfect example of a medieval feudal castle surrounded by a moat. The western walls are a sheer drop of 50 metres into the Rhône. The royal dwellings, minstrel gallery (René was keen on minstrels and troubadours), banqueting hall, cour d'honneur, chapel and stone stairways should all be seen. Despite the wars of religion, Richelieu, the revolutionary citoyens, the Allies' bombardment of 1944, and even the Wehrmacht, this beautiful castle survives intact (as a prison until 1926!). It is closed on Tuesday.

A fifth-century sarcophagus is reputed to be the tomb of Ste Marthe in the crypt of the little church opposite the château. Although sadly damaged by bombing, the little church still attracts pilgrims.

The seventeenth-century Town Hall and fifteenth-century arcaded houses in the Rue des Halles are close to the Tourist Office, housed in a handsome old building in the Ave. de la République, tel. 90-91-03-52. Alphonse Daudet made fun of the Provençaux in his novel *Tartarin de Tarascon* published in 1862. Daudet's shooting expedition took place in the hills just north of Tarascon called La Montagnette. On our last visit to Tarascon a circus had been pitched between the castle and the road bridge across the Rhône. A large dun-coloured dromedary was busy tearing up and eating the Council's shrubs. I think Daudet might have been amused.

Tarascon is for most of the year a quiet, sleepy provincial town well placed for excursions to the Abbey of Montmajour, Fontvielle, Les Baux, St Rémy, Maillanne (Mistral's museum) and the fine, dignified working abbey of St Michel-de-Frigolet in the north.

On the first Sunday in May a great pilgrimage takes place at the eleventh-century Romanesque Chapel of Notre-Dame-de-Château, 8 km SE of Tarascon. And on 1 June a bucolic pilgrimage is held in Boulbon, 8 km NE of Tarascon (just beyond the Abbey of St Michel-de-Frigolet) – the procession *des fioles* (bottle procession), in honour of the Roman priest Marcellin. In 304 AD he was martyred in Rome. A bottle of his blood turned into wine and in due course he was canonised and became the patron saint of wine. In the Romanesque chapel in Boulbon are two reliquaries of the saint. Local wine growers bring bottles to be blessed, which are then kept to ward off fever and illness.

There are several modest hotels in Tarascon. Le Provençal is at 12 Cours Aristide Briand, tel. 90-91-11-41. Try their *jambon cru de Provence* and *truite belle meunière* on the 53-franc menu. The Hôtel du Pont, 2 Ave. de la République, tel. 90-91-39-24 and the Hôtel du Rhône, Place Colonel Berrurier, tel. 90-91-03-35, are also worth trying. All have easy parking facilities.

CHAPTER NINETEEN: AVIGNON

Avignon is one of the seven wonders of France. It is famous for its poetic bridge of St Bénézet, and the Court of Splendour and Magnificence of the fourteenth-century Popes, which overlooks the mightly Rhône. Bounded on the north and west sides by the river, the old town lies in a plain surrounded by 5 km of ramparts and covers an area of about 700 square metres. All the main sights, therefore, are in easy walking distance of your hotel.

The history of Avignon

Roads lead to Avignon from Villeneuve-les-Avignon (across the bridge Pont Edouard Daladier), from Nîmes (the N100), from Arles (the N570), from Aix (N7), and from Carpentras (N107). It is easy to see that the confluence of these roads and the river traffic on the Rhône has made Avignon prosperous and now; with a population of nearly 100,000, it is the préfecture town of the department of the Vaucluse. The medieval fairs of Avignon and neighbouring Beaucaire, and the fact that the town was made a sanctuary from the law, brought an extraordinary collection of travellers to Avignon. There were bands of brothers (mendicant friars of six orders), persecuted Jews, smugglers and forgers, painters and musicians who all needed hotels, cafés, restaurants, brothels and bawdy houses. No wonder that Avignon became notorious when the Popes and their scores of Cardinals held sway in the fourteenth-century Palais des Papes. Later the town became a refuge for English political and religious exiles, including many Jacobites.

Few signs of the Emperor Hadrian's Roman colony remain. The Place de l'Horloge was the original forum, but Avignon remains a classic city of the Middle Ages. The Bénézet bridge was started in 1177 and fortified in the fifteenth century. The two great fortified Palaces, described by Jean Froissart as 'The most beautiful and the strongest houses in the world', were completed in the mid-fourteenth century. (Benedict XII constructed the Old Palace and Clement VI the New Palace.) The gold-coloured ramparts were erected by the Popes also in the fourteenth century (and restored in the nineteenth century by Viollet-le-Duc). The Cathedral Notre-Dame-des-Doms was built in the twelfth century but remodelled in the fourteenth century, as was the clock tower in the Place de l'Horloge, and the churches of St Symphorien, St Pierre, St Didier and St Agricol. The many medieval houses include the chapels of the Black, White and the Grey Penitents and Cardinal Ceccano's Tower (now the public library). It takes little effort to imagine Daudet's description of Avignon,

'Without rival for gaiety and endless feasting. Cardinals sailed up the Rhône in stately barges bedecked with wind-tossed banners, the Papal guards sang Latin chants in the squares, the mendicant friars prattled ceaselessly and all the houses, thronging like bees round the great palace, hummed with constant activity of all kinds . . .'

Amidst all this physical activity the Papal court created wealth which in turn attracted painters, architects, sculptors, printers, glass-blowers (still there in the Rue de Limas) and tapestry makers. The Avignon school of primitive painters is described in another chapter. The works of Joseph Vernet and Hubert Robert can be seen in the Calvet Museum. Avignon survived the horrors of the Albigensian crusade (1220), the Black Death which killed 9 cardinals and 17,000 citizens, the Great Schism (when there were two Popes), the religious wars of the sixteenth century and the French Revolution. The beautiful Palace was then a barracks and a prison so the worthy *citoyens* destroyed the furnishings but not the buildings. In October 1791, sixty people were murdered by the revolutionaries in the Tour de la Glacière in the Pope's Palace. Madame Guillotine has a lot to answer for!

Places to visit

Start your city visit with a mandatory conducted tour (22 francs) of the Papal Palace which is open every day, but closed for lunch 12–2 p.m. Tours are on the hour and take an hour. You will need a lot of imagination to fill the huge empty rooms with their fourteenth-century frenzied activity – the two audience chambers, Clementine, St Martin's and St John's chapels, the Benedict XII cloister, the Grand Tinel banqueting hall, Grand Council Chamber and the smaller Papal bedchamber, Stag room and Robing room.

On one side of the huge cobbled square – the Place du Palais – is the Notre-Dame-des-Doms Cathedral. In 1345 the English sculptor H. Wilfred helped decorate this Romanesque church. Look for the tombs of two of the Avignon Popes. Two hundred metres north is the Petit Palais Museum (closed Tuesday) with the Avignon school of Enguerrand Quartron and Josse Lieferinxe represented, although the majority of paintings are Italian (the Campana di Cavelli collection). A five-minute walk up steps and paths will take you to the Rocher-des-Doms, a terraced public garden around a lake with superb views of the Rhône, St Bénézet Bridge and the mountain ranges of Ventoux and Luberon. This is a good place for a lunchtime picnic.

The Rue de la République is the main street, running 1 km north to south from the Petit Palais to the SNCF station. Halfway down is the Tourist Office (41 Cours Jean-Jaurès, tel. 90-82-65-11) and, in the same building, the Wine Offices of the Vaucluse department. The old Mint erected in 1619 by Cardinal Borghese, now the Music Conservatory, is a handsome building opposite the Pope's Palace and 200 metres from the fourteenth-century clock tower and Hôtel de Ville.

Avignon has many fine museums. Besides the Petit Palais, there is the Calvet Museum (closed Tuesday), 200 metres west of the Ave. de la République. This eighteenth-century mansion has a balanced art collection including Avignon art of Nicolas Mignard (and Impressionists), as well as local prehistory, Roman antiquities and a wrought iron collection. Some of the finest works of Breughel, Bosch and Vasarely can be seen here. The Lapidary Museum next door (closed Tuesday), with sculptures and stone carvings, is near the Tourist Office. Try also to visit the Theodore Aubanel Museum (he was co-founder with Mistral of the Provençal Félibrige society), the Louis Voulard Museum (faience, furnishings, tapestries and Far Eastern collection), Requien Museum (botany and local natural history), and the Roure Palace (in a fifteenth-century mansion of the Baroncelli family).

The many old town houses or mansions are to be found in the Rue de la Masse, Rue du Roi René, Rue Dorée and Crillon Square. The mendicant friars' chapels are in the Rue Banasterie (Black), Place de la Principale (White) and Rue des Teinturies (Grey). Try to imagine the thirteenth-century confréries dressed in sackcloth robes (coloured according to their brotherhood) and twisted rope girdles flocking the cobbled streets of Avignon. There were also Blue, Violet and Red penitents. The White were the smartest and the Red were working-class penitents! The Revolution killed off most of the brotherhoods, although the Black lasted until 1948 and the Grey Penitents still continue. The streets of Avignon are well worth careful exploration. There is a memento of its medieval past on every corner, including trades such as cloth-dying and basket-weaving (banastiers).

Local festivals

Avignon has a major summer festival from early July to early August, with concerts, plays, films, dance, mime and folklore parades. There are 12 different official venues and a fringe festival with 35 locations! There are also jazz concerts in the Place Grillon and street theatre in the Place de l'Horloge.

On Bastille day, Avignon has a major fireworks display. There is a bric-à-brac fair, 31 August–3 September; Grand prix horse races at Ascension and Pentecost; a spring fair; St André's fair on 30 November – never a dull moment! One useful address is that of Arts Baroques en Provence, 37 Rue St Jean-le-Vieux, tel. 90-86-88-04, who organise classical concerts in 16 towns and cities in Provence.

Hotels and restaurants

The best hotel in Avignon is the Europe in a sixteenth-century mansion in the Place Grillon, but the best budget hotels are in the Rue Agricol Perdiguier on the east side of the Ave. de la République near the Convent of the Celestins. Here you will find the Splendid at No. 17, tel. 90-86-14-46, du Parc at No. 18, tel. 90-82-71-55 and Pacific at No. 7. In the Rue Joseph Vernet, west of the Ave. de la République near the Calvet Museum, are the Hôtel Innova at No. 100, tel. 90-82-54-10 and the Mignon at No. 12, tel. 90-82-17-30.

Good-value restaurants are Flunch, 11 Bd. Raspail (near the Chamber of Commerce), Le Magnanen, 14 Rue Portail-Magnanen (near the station), and Le Patio, 2 Rue Petite Calade (off Rue Joseph Vernet). If money is no object, go to Hiély, 5 Rue de la République or La Fourchette, 7 Rue Racine (run by Robert Hiély).

On the river

The best views of Avignon are from the river. Prosper Merimée, Frédéric Mistral and Charles Dickens have all written of their delight at seeing the town for the first time as they sailed south from Pont St Esprit.

Just beside the Pont Edouard Daladier is the quay where Mireio boats leave for a variety of river tours. Les Grands Bateaux de Provence, tel. 90-85-62-25, have sophisticated boats for 250 passengers with a restaurant, cabaret and dancing on board. Arles is one of the destinations, Roquemaure another. Another alternative is Le Cygne, a smaller boat which takes 50 passengers and starts at the Quai de la Ligne, 300 metres north of the Pont d'Avignon, tel. 66-59-35-62. This offers trips to the Camargue and Aigues-Mortes.

Excursions are many and varied. Across the bridge to the west is Villeneuve-les-Avignon where the wealthy Cardinals built their palaces, the Carthusian Hospice or monastery Val de Bénédiction (where there is a remarkable Enguerrand Charonton *Coronation of the Virgin* painted in 1453), Jean-le-Bon's Fort St-André built in 1360, the fourteenth-century Tour de Philippe le Bel, and the fourteenth-century Church of Notre-Dame. The Hôtel de l'Atelier, 5 Rue de la Foire, tel. 90-25-01-84, is good value.

The Roman aqueduct Pont-du-Gard is 25 km to the west on the N100, the Abbey of St Michel-de-Frigolet 15 km SW on the D35. The *rosé* wine villages of Tavel and Lirac are 20 km NW on the N580. Châteauneuf-du-Pape vineyards are 20 km north on the D183/D17, and the grotto of Thouzon at Le Thor is 20 km east on the N100. Cavaillon, the fruit and vegetable market town of Provence (pop. 21,000) in the River Durance valley, is 30 km SE on the D973.

CHAPTER TWENTY:
ORANGE

In the Vaucluse department 30 km north of Avignon is the old Roman town once called Arausio. Now large and prosperous with 27,500 inhabitants, Orange is on the N7 and is the second largest town in the department. It has two outstanding Roman antiquities and is the centre of the wine-growing area, with Châteauneuf-du-Pape to the south, Tavel and Lirac to the SW and Gigondas and Vacqueyras to the east. Along with Carpentras, it is a major fruit- and vegetable-growing area, particularly tomatoes, strawberries, aubergines and melons.

Local history

Hannibal and his elephants passed close to Arausio in 218 BC before crossing the Alps during the Second Punic War. Orange was colonised in 36 BC by Emperor Augustus' second legion, after which the Romans built temples, baths, a circus, gymnasium, arena and theatre as well as a massive commemorative arch. After the Romans left, the Barbarians repeatedly sacked the town. In 1274 Orange became a small principality within the Comtat Venaissin. This was the area between the River Durance, Mount Ventoux and the Rhône which was handed over to the Papal Holy See. Pernes-les-Fontaines and then Carpentras were the capitals of this strange little enclave, until in the sixteenth century it became part of the Netherlands 'empire' and during 1689-1702 was owned by the Anglo-Dutch monarchy! During the religious wars Orange became a Huguenot community and in 1562 it was sacked by the Catholics.

During the French Revolution 332 citizens (including 37 monks) were guillotined in the Cours Aristide-Briand (just outside the present Tourist Office). Now it is a peaceful, pleasant town, the more so since the A7, the Autoroute de Soleil, has creamed off traffic from the N7.

The methodical Prince Maurice of Nassau fortified his city of Orange in 1622. Unfortunately for posterity, he used stones from the Roman antiquities not only for new defensive ramparts but also to build his own château on the hill of St Eutrope on the south side of town. So the Roman temples, baths and arena disappeared. The Musée de la Ville, on the Place Mounet, opposite the Roman theatre, is worth a visit.

Two links with Britain can be seen. In a courtyard amongst the sarcophagi and fragments of Roman columns is a stone coat of arms of England — presumably a legacy of William of Orange. On the second floor there is a collection of Sir Frank Brangwyn's paintings presented by a Monsieur E. Daladier to the town.

Emperor Hadrian's Roman theatre is the best preserved in the world. It could hold 9,000 spectators in tiered seats in three different sections. Forty metres high and one hundred long, it is the same size as that in Arles. King Louis XIV described it as 'the finest wall in my kingdom'. He then ordered the destruction of the château and the town ramparts in case the Protestants became a threat! The theatre (entrance costs 15 francs) has been discreetly restored since being used as a criminal prison and the town refuse-dump in the nineteenth century. A gymnasium, sports ground and three small temples (to Jupiter, Juno and Minerva) are part of this complex dominated by the reassembled statue of Emperor Augustus in the central alcove of the theatre. He would probably have approved of the summer festivals of music and drama now performed each year.

The second grand Roman monument is the so-called Arc de Triumph, which is situated a quarter of an hour's walk due north of the theatre on the road to Lyon (continuation of the Rue Victor Hugo). It is a commemorative triple-arched monument, the third largest in existence, and celebrates the exploits of the Roman Second Legion with victories over the Gauls and the Massiliot Greek fleet. It was built about 25 AD and is therefore a century or more older than the theatre. It stood proudly at the entrance of the Roman town, at a height of nearly 20 metres, a rectangular shape of 20 metres in width and 8.5 metres in depth. Now it is in the middle of a little island in the centre of the N7.

Local festivals

In 1869 two art lovers, Antony Real and Felix Ripert, started a theatrical group. Orange became a musical town and ever since 'les Chorégies' have been famous. Throughout June–July there are musical concerts and operas (often Wagner) and folklore contests usually in the Théâtre Antique. Towards the end of March there is a two-day Carnival with processions, floats, fireworks and dancing in the streets. At the end of May is a three-day Fête du Printemps, and at the end of August a three-day festival to celebrate their twinning *(jumelage)* with seven overseas towns (but none in the UK). Contact the Maison du Théâtre, Place des Frères-Mounet, tel. 90-34-15-52, for information. Wine fairs take place in Orange twice a year in the summer and winter.

Places to visit

The Tourist Office is on the Cours Aristide-Briand, tel. 90-34-70-88 on the corner of the main square on the west side of town (with easy parking).

The Tourist Office recommend a morning's walking tour of the old town and in the summer season guided tours start at 10.30 a.m. (tariff 15 francs). There are many shady little squares with fountains and a new pedestrian precinct. There is little else to see in Orange. The Orange Nassau château is in ruins, the erstwhile Cathedral of Notre-Dame of Nazareth is on the site of the twelfth-century pagan temple to Diana, but there are delightful views from the St Eutrope hill (near the open air swimming pool and municipal camping site of Le Jonquier).

Hotels and restaurants

The Hôtel Arènes, Place de Langes, is the best hotel. There are three budget hotels near the Place aux Herbes in the pedestrian centre: the St Florent, 4 Rue du Mazeau, tel. 90-34-18-53; Arcotel (originally Père Tranquille), Place aux Herbes, tel. 90-34-09-23, and the Freau, 13 Rue Ancien College, tel. 90-34-06-26. Try also Le Français, 21 Ave. Frédéric Mistral, tel. 90-34-67-65.

In the Place de la République next to the excellent fromagerie La Populaire ('Chevrotons de Provence') is the restaurant La Sangria. Le Provençal in 27 Rue de la République; the Arausio (near the Tourist Office); and Ma Cuisine, 4 Rue de Renoyer (at Place Clemenceau) all have good-value meals in the 50-60 franc range.

Touring

Local excursions off the beaten track suggested by the Tourist Office are: SW on the D17, 6 km to Caderousse on the Rhône banks (with château and chapel of the Dukes of Gramont, eleventh-century Gothic church, tenth-century Romanesque chapel of St Martin). You can also go to Camaret (pop. 2,500), 6 km on the D975, the 'castra marii' of the Consul Marius of 102 BC, with an unusual clock tower in the ramparts or to Gigondas (*Caveau de degustation* in Place du Portail, tel. 90-65-85-53, where you can taste and buy any of 50 different wines). Piolenc, 7 km north on the N7 (pop. 3,700), has a garlic fête with floats, wine tasting and a horse fair during the last weekend of August. In Serignan, 6 km NE from Orange on the D976, there is a wine co-op, entomological museum and medieval fête called *la grappe d'or*, each 5–10 August. Travaillan, 9 km (just beyond Camaret), or the Uchaux and Violes wine villages north and east of Orange are also worth visiting. Violes also has a flying club, and hunting and fishing facilities.

CHAPTER TWENTY-ONE: NÎMES

Technically Nîmes is in the Languedoc, but it is so close to Avignon, Arles and the Camargue, and was so much a key part of Roman Provincia, that I have included it. The Autoroute A9 thunders past on the south side from Orange to Montpellier and the N113 bisects the town from Arles in the SE to Alès in the NW. Unusually there is no river, but a spring flows from the Jardin de la Fontaine gently in a canal through part of the town. The Celtic god of the spring Nemausus gave his name to the capital of a Belgic tribe, the Arecomic Volcans.

Local history

When Anthony was defeated by Octavius, Roman veterans (with their symbol of a crocodile and palm tree) settled here. The crossroads of the Via Domitia and the road leading to the Cevennes, and the relationship between Colonia Augusta Nemausus and Rome, soon made for prosperity. The classic Maison Carrée with its Greek architectural style was originally dedicated to Augustus' grandsons. A perfect rectangle, it is 26 metres long and 13 metres wide and was built in 100 BC. It overlooked the forum, and was known originally as the Capitol. The Tourist Office is 100 metres away, at 6 Rue Auguste, tel. 66-67-29-11.

Places to visit

To the northwest, ten minutes' walk past the Place Aristide Briand, are the elegant Jardins de la Fontaine. These are now

formal water gardens enveloping a rather ruined Temple of
Diana, a tall watchtower on three floors also built in 100 BC
called the Tour Magne (with superb views) and elegant
balustrades, pools, and tree-lined alleyways — a perfect
backdrop for assignations and summer concerts. On our last
visit we talked to the swans, listened to the music, and there
was a *boules* contest for scores of veteran *boulistes* in the
Jardins. But the main Nîmois crowds were sauntering in their
hundreds to watch a Spanish bullfight in the last of the major
Roman monuments — the amphitheatre.

It is situated in the Place des Arènes at the south end of
Bd. Victor Hugo. It is the best preserved of any Roman arena,
dates from 50 AD and is almost identical to that in Arles,
although a little smaller, and designed by the same architect.
Once it held 21,000 spectators and now at Whitsun the
Spanish matadors perform to the same number as they
despatch their bulls (but no lions or Christians). The
measurements are amazing — a height of 20 metres, two
stories of arches and 130 × 100 metres in length and in
width.

The other Roman antiquities to be seen include the unique
Castellum, a curious basin with ten small holes that controlled
input of water from five canals to those parts of the city
allocated water resources. It is situated in the Rue du Fort,
north of the Bd. Gambetta. And in the Musée des Antiquités
are the statues of the Venus de Nîmes and of Apollo (with
a quiver of arrows) and some superb Roman mosaics. Finally,
the Porte d'Arles is a Roman city gate of Caesar Augustus'
reign opposite the church of St Baudile in the Place des
Carmes. A combined ticket should be purchased to see the
four famous Roman sites — Maison Carrée, amphithéâtre,
Tour Magne and Temple of Diana.

The Tourist Office publish a useful leaflet, *Rendez Vous à
Nîmes*. They have also devised a sensible and interesting walk
through the old town, to see the Bishop's Palace, Hôtel de
Ville, the Cathedral of Notre-Dame and St Castor, and a score
of fine fifteenth- to eighteenth-century town mansions. Many
of these can be seen in the Rue Dorée, Rue du Chapitre or
Rue de Bernis. In the Place des Herbes you will find an exotic

array of fruits and vegetables, including stalls with 23 varieties of local olives.

The museums in Nîmes are quite close together: the Natural History and Archeology, and the Old Nîmes (which has interesting bullfighting memorabilia). The Beaux Arts is five minutes' walk south of the arena with a good collection of the French school to be seen.

Local markets and festivals

The markets are usually held on Monday morning in the Avenue Jean-Jaurès; Tuesday morning in the Ave. Bir Hakeim; Thursday morning in the Ave. des Arts Banlieu; and Friday morning, Ave. Jean-Jaurès. For visitors, some of the interesting events are the spring fair at the end of March; the Fair of St Michel on 29 September; and the Exhibition Artisans d'Art, 5–13 November. The Nîmes Opéra is at 1 Place de la Calade, the Théâtre Populaire du Midi at 21 Rue F. Pelloutier and the little café-theatre, Titoit de Titus, is at 6 Rue Titus.

During the third week in July the International Jazz Festival is held with world-famous stars. Opera is performed in the arena and concerts in the Temple of Diana. Incidentally, for any readers who would be interested to become bullfighters, France's only school of bullfighting (L'Ecole Française de Tauromachie, 57 Rue Roussy, tel. 66-76-04-65) will, for a fee, teach you the finer arts.

Hotels and restaurants

There are several inexpensive hotels, including the Majestic, 10 Rue Pradier, tel. 66-29-24-14; the France, 4 Bd. des Arènes, tel. 66-67-47-72; and the Modern, 10 Rue Roussy, tel. 66-67-29-27. There are, of course, many good restaurants. We liked the *coquille nîmoise brandade* at Au Bec Fin, 11 Rue Nationale; or try Le Cigalon, 11 Rue Xavier Sigalon, where the Provençal fish dishes are good. Les Hirondelles, 13 Rue Bigot also has good menus.

On a lighter note, try the local *confiserie; dragées* at Maison

Bez, 1860 Rue Naturale; *croquant villaret*, a round almond biscuit; or *caladon*, another local variety.

Touring

Nîmes and Aix-en-Provence are the same size, with populations of about 130,000 but their styles are quite different. Nîmes, part of Languedoc, has the superb Roman sights and a lusty, earthy ambience. But Aix-en-Provence has cool elegance and intellectual status!

Nîmes is the centre of many intriguing excursions easily reached by car. To the south is Aigues-Mortes, the fishing port-resort of Le Grau-du-Roi and the Perrier water lake and factory. To the SE lies Arles and the Camargue, to the east Beaucaire and Tarascon and to the NE the *rosé* wine areas of Tavel and Lirac. There is also the outstanding Roman aqueduct called the Pont-du-Gard tucked away in a sleepy valley 20 km north off the D981. We took a picnic lunch and gazed and gazed at this incredible monument to Roman engineering − 2,000 years ago several thousand slaves were chivvied into building a water channel cross-country in a straight line for a distance of 50 km! Caesar Augustus wanted pure water from a guaranteed source near Uzès supplied to the Castellum in Nîmes. The problems were immense as there were, and are, many river valleys along the line selected. The Pont-du-Gard, across the River Gard, is nearly 300 metres in length and 50 metres in height. The three magnificent tiers can be crossed on foot. You can also cross inside the top covered canal if you so wish, at no charge except parking fees. There are two *auberges* for visitors who want to see this amazing Roman site in style, the Vieux Moulin and Le Colombier. Both have rooms, restaurants and views of the huge yellow-gold stones that make up the bridge, the beautiful green flowing river with white sandy beaches on both sides and buzzards circling above the valley.

CHAPTER TWENTY-TWO:
THE WINES OF PROVENCE

Some of the best red and *rosé* wines of France are grown in Provence. Not only are they much appreciated in the region but many are exported to the UK market. Wines have been grown in Provence for 2,500 years in ideal conditions so they ought to be good! The principal Appellations Controllées (A.O.C.) are as follows:

Vaucluse wines

In the southern Rhône valley in the Vaucluse, the famous names include Châteauneuf-du-Pape, Gigondas and Vacqueyras − intense and powerful red wines often of 14 degrees of alcohol (10 or 10.5 is the norm for most table wines), the grapes for which are grown just north-east of Avignon.

Beaumes-de-Venise, a pinkish-golden nectar, is a sweet muscat wine of 15 degrees which is ideal to go with British puddings and sweets. Rasteau is a fortified (alcohol added) red, white or *rosé* from the sloping southern vineyards near Vaison-la-Romaine. Rasteau wines can be kept for several years.

Just across the River Rhône to the west, in the department of the Gard, are two soft and delicate *rosé* wines. Tavel is described as fruity and lively, its shimmering, pink hues are tinged with ruby and topaz and its floral aroma suggests wild strawberries. No wonder it is France's No. 1 *rosé* wine! A few km NE is Lirac, grown on extremely stony stoil − a good *rosé* but not quite so famous as its neighbour. Lirac ruby reds and dry whites are also produced.

However, 80 per cent of the production in the southern Rhône valley is the basic *appellation* from 162 communes of

Côtes du Rhône, mostly red, but also white and a little *rosé*.

There is also Côtes du Rhône-Villages from 17 villages — a slightly better quality than ordinary Côtes du Rhône.

At the foot of the Mont Ventoux, still in the Vaucluse department, are the wines Côtes du Ventoux A.O.C., once known as *'vin de café'* (a very light red wine). The Côtes du Luberon V.D.Q.S. (Vin Délimité de Qualité Superieure) are red, dry white and *rosé* wines grown to the east of Avignon. Finally, the Vins de Pays du Vaucluse are also red, dry white and *rosé* wines mostly grown in the south of the department and drunk locally.

Bouches-du-Rhône wines

Now take a deep breath whilst we look at the wines grown in the Mediterranean department of Bouches-du-Rhône:

- **Bandol** A.O.C. red, dry white and *rosé* wines from terraced vineyards between La Ciotat and Toulon have a very fine reputation.

- **Cassis** A.O.C. is grown around the port of that name.

- **Palette** A.O.C. is a small *apellation* south of Aix-en-Provence.

- **Côteaux d'Aix-en-Provence** V.D.Q.S. is grown south and east of Aix.

- **Coteaux des Baux-en-Provence** V.D.Q.S. are grown near St Rémy-de-Provence.

- **Petite Crau** *vins de pays* are also grown near St Rémy-de-Provence. Vins de Pays des Bouches-du-Rhône are grown throughout the department. There is a huge A.O.C. called Côtes de Provence which spreads from a large crescent shape east of Aix, plus an area north of La Ciotat. The main area is in the neighbouring Var department east of Toulon to St Raphael.

Annual production figures

To get this substantial wine area into perspective I have assembled some annual production figures.

1. **Châteauneuf-du-Pape A.O.C.** Production each year is of about 14 million bottles from no less than 13 different grape varieties including Grenache, Syrah, Mourvedre, and Cinsault. This robust, hearty, full-coloured red wine has lots of tannin and can age happily for 10–15 years. Only 3 per cent of the production is white. Thirty-five producers offer tasting facilities from the vineyards scattered over 3,000 hectares. One can also taste at the Association of Prestige and Tradition, Rue de la République, tel. 90-83-72-29. Since demand is so strong there is no need for a local co-op for Châteauneuf-du-Pape wines, although the co-op at Courthezon, called Le Cellier des Princes, offers an inexpensive blend. In the small town of Châteauneuf (pop. 2,000), the ruined castle on top of the hill is an ideal destination for a walk after a good lunch at Les Frères Jacques, Rue Commandant Lemaitre, or Le Logis d'Arnavel, 3 km away on the D17.

2. **Gigondas A.O.C.** This was made an appellation in 1971. Production is 5 million bottles a year from 1,100 hectares, and the red or *rosé* wine (almost as good as the best Châteauneuf-du-Pape) has to be made from 65 per cent the Grenache grape and at least 25 per cent of Syrah, Mourvedre and Cinsault. There are 15 growers offering tasting facilities but my advice is to visit the communal cave in the small main square where all their wines can be tasted and purchased by the bottle, so that you can select your own – the Cave des Vignerons, tel. 90-65-86-27. The nearest hotel is Les Florets, 1½ km away, tel. 90-65-85-01.

3. **Vacqueyras V.D.Q.S.** This has the best Côtes du Rhône-Villages red wines (out of 17 villages) and is nearly as good as the neighbouring Châteauneuf-de-Pape and Gigondas. It is made by 12 growers from the same grapes too. Production is rather less than Gigondas. My advice is to visit the excellent modern co-op, Cave du Troubadour, at Vacqueyras, tel. 90-65-84-54 and there taste and buy not only Vacqueyras but Gigondas as well. They have 125 local farmers who are grouped together to make this fine wine.

129

4. **Rasteau V.D.N.** This is the fortified wine made by nine producers from the Grenache grape with pure wine alcohol added to bring the strength up to 21.5°. Aged in the cask for several years, the flavour of the deep gold or tawny wine is called 'Rancio' (not to be confused with rancid!). It is a rare and excellent wine from the co-op (2O km NE of Orange).

5. **Tavel A.O.C.** In the Gard department is a dry rosé made from the Grenache grape with a little Cinsault added. Over 5 million bottles are made each year of this most famous French rosé wine. Vineyards cover 836 hectares. There are 15 growers with tasting facilities, including the co-op, tel. 90-50-03-57.

6. **Lirac A.O.C.** In the Gard close to Tavel, Lirac produces red and white wines as well as rosé (nearly as good as Tavel). The Grenache grape must account for at least 40 per cent. Production is 3 million bottles a year. The Château de Segries, tel. 66-21-85-35, offers tasting facilities. Lirac has produced wines since the sixteenth century from the villages of Roquemaure, St Laurent des Arbres and St Genies de Comolas.

7. **Beaumes-de-Venise V.D.N.** Wine known as 'vin doux naturel' is made from a grape called 'muscat de Frontignan' to produce, with added alcohol, a strength of 21.5°. The pale-golden wine with strong perfume, drunk chilled, is excellent as an aperitif or dessert wine. Production is 1 million bottles, mainly from the Cave co-op, tel. 90-62-94-45.

8. **The Côtes du Rhône Villages A.O.C.** The production of this wine is 15 million bottles a year, mainly from the Grenache grape (65 per cent), Carignan (10 per cent) and the cépages nobles of Mourvedre, Syrah and Cinsault must amount to 25 per cent. Mainly red, but also rosé and white wines are produced from 17 villages. These are Beaumes-de-Venise, Cairanne (cave co-op des Coteaux, tel. 90-30-82-05), Chusclan, Laudun, Rasteau, Roaix, Rochegude, Rousset (in the Drome with the co-op

in Quartier St Joseph also making Marc de Provence), Sablet (co-op tel. 90-36-90-20), St Gervais (in the Gard), St Maurice-sur-Eygues, St Pantaleon-les-Vignes (near Rousset), Seguret (shares co-op with Roaix), Vacqueyras, Valréas, Vinsobres and Visan. The last three are in the north and Valréas has two co-ops and Visan one. I have listed these 17 villages because Côtes du Rhône-Villages (and each village tags its name on to this description) are usually inexpensive, good-value wines. The local co-op will be pleased to see you but good manners suggest that you buy some bottles after your tasting.

9. **Côtes du Ventoux A.O.C.** This area of 6,400 hectares of vineyards produces 18 million bottles, mainly of red wines and usually good value. Taste them at the co-op in Apt called Le Vin de Sylla, tel. 90-74-05-39; at Beaumont-de-Ventoux co-op, tel. 90-65-11-78; at Caromb, Cave St Marc, tel. 90-62-40-24; at Goult Lumière (near Gordes), tel. 90-72-20-04; at Maubec-Coustellet (two co-ops); at Mormoiron *les roches blanches*, tel. 90-61-80-07; at Mazan, tel. 90-69-70-31; at Pernes-les-Fontaines, tel. 90-66-59-48; at Puymeras, tel. 90-46-40-78; at La Tour d'Aigues, tel. 90-77-40-65; at St Didier, La Courtoise, tel. 90-66-01-15; at Le Thor, tel. 90-22-20-43; at Villes-sur-Auzon, La Montagne Rouge, tel. 90-61-82-08; and at Vaison-la-Romaine, tel. 90-36-00-43. Suitable towns at which to stay are Apt, Sault, Carpentras or Vaison. A tour of the Mont Ventoux region interspersed with visits to the local wine co-ops has great potential!

10. **Côtes du Luberon V.D.Q.S.** These wines are grown on the right bank of the Durance River in the Vaucluse, east of Avignon. The reds are similar to the Côtes du Ventoux in style with a soft, ripe, fruity finish. The towns and villages to visit are Apt, Cadenet, Cucuron, Grambois, Lauris, Cavaillon (175 Ave. Germain Chauvin, tel. 90-71-01-79), La Motte d'Aigues, Lourmarin, Maubec and La Tour d'Aigues (two co-ops). No less then 35 communes, with 2,850 hectares, produce 9 million bottles a year.

11. **Côtes du Rhône** This huge appellation was created in 1937 and spans six departments. The 41,000 hectares produce well over 200 million bottles, much of it *vin ordinaire*. Occasionally a high-class château can be found, such as Château St Esteve of Uchaux (near Orange); La Reuiscoulado, owned by Jean Trintignant, near Châteauneuf-du-Pape; Domaine Rabasse-Chavarin of Les Côteaux-St-Martin, Cairanne; or Domaine Palestor la Fagotière near Orange.

Names to look for

Before we leave the Vaucluse and Gard regions I am including a short list of châteaux names for each area which the wine experts say are really very good indeed!

● **Châteauneuf-du-Pape:** Château de Beaucastel; Domaine de Cabrières les Silex; Cuvée du Vatican from Diffonty; Château Fortia; Château de la Gardine; Domaine du Clos des Papes (from Paul Avril); Domaine de la Roquette; and Domaine Trintignant.

● **Gigondas:** Domaine Raspail-Ay; Domaine du Pesquier; and Domaine du Clos des Cazeaux.

● **Vacqueyras:** Le Sang des Cailloux.

● **Tavel:** Domaine de la Forcadière; Domaine de Roc Epine; and Prieure de Montezargues.

● **Lirac:** Domaine de la Tour; Château de Bouchassy.

● **Rasteau:** Domaine de la Soumade.

● **Côtes du Luberon:** Château de l'Isolette (near Apt).

● **Côtes du Rhône-Villages;** Domaine de Cabasse (near Seguret); Domaine Clos des Cazeaux (near Vacqueyras); Domaine Rabasse-Charavin (Cairanne); Domaine de Wilfried (Rasteau).

Coastal wine regions

Further south in the Bouches-du-Rhône department we come to the coastal wine regions.

1. **Bandol A.O.C.** Three million bottles are produced each year here, mainly red and *rosé* wines from the Mourvedre grape (at least 50 per cent) and the rest from Cinsault and Grenache. The small white production of 150,000 bottles is made from Clairette and Ugni Blanc grapes. A good soft spicy red, Bandol can age happily for 20 years! Noted growers are Château de Cagueloup (St Cyr-sur-Mer), Moulin des Costes (La Cadière-d'Azur), Domaine de l'Hermitage (Le Beausset), Domaine Lafran-Veyrolles (La Cadière-d'Azur), Domaine de la Laidière (Le Beausset) and Château Pradeaux (St Cyr-sur-Mer).

2. **Cassis A.O.C.** This is a small *appellation* of only 200 hectares producing 700,000 bottles a year, half of white from the Clairette and Ugni Blanc grapes, and half red/*rosé* from Grenache, Cinsault, Mourvedre and Carignan. The whites are dry and pale yellow in colour, smell of rosemary and myrtle and should be drunk young. Clos Boulard and Château de Fontblanche are two good vineyards. Given A.O.C. status in 1936, the 13 vignerons carry on a long tradition of quality wines made since the twelfth century.

3. **Palette A.O.C.** This is a small *appellation* between Aix-en-Provence and the Abbey of Tholonet. Only 100,000 bottles are produced and most are drunk locally. The Château Simone produces good *rosé*.

4. **Coteaux d'Aix-en-Provence V.D.Q.S.** This is a large *appellation* of 3,000 hectares south and east of Aix. Production is 14 million bottles, of which 95 per cent is red/*rosé* from the usual four grapes, plus Cabernet Sauvignon and Syrah. Best growers are Château Vignelaure (near Rians), Château la Coste (Le Puy Sainte-Reparade) and Château de Calissanne (Port Marly in the Var department). There are co-ops at Aix (Les Granettes, Route de Berre, tel. 42-20-19-88); at Berre l'Etang; Eguilles; Lambesc; Lançon de Provence; La Fare des Oliviers; Pelissanne; Le Puy Sainte-Reparade; Senas; St Cannat.

5. **Coteaux des Baux-en-Provence V.D.Q.S.** This is a small *appellation* near St Rémy-de-Provence, Fontvieille and

Les Baux-de-Provence. The red is well worth looking for, similar to the Coteaux d'Aix.

6. **Petite Crau** These wines are grown near St Rémy-de-Provence and are similar to (5) above. There is little white, but the red and *rosé* are reasonable. Try the co-op at Noves, tel. 90-91-01-30, and Graveson, tel. 90-95-71-12.

7. **Côtes de Provence A.O.C.** This is a huge *appellation*, mostly in the Var department, of 90 million bottles from 18,000 hectares. Whites account for only 10 per cent. The reds and *rosés* vary from very good to indifferent and are made from the Grenache, Cinsault, Mourvèdre and Carignan grapes. Cabernet Sauvignon and Syrah can be added to upgrade the quality. All the wines should be drunk chilled. The Phoenicians planted vines here 600 years BC and the Romans, including Julius Caesar, took a keen interest in them. They achieved A.O.C. status in 1977. The best châteaux within reach of Marseille or Aix-en-Provence are: Château Grand Boise (near Trets); Mas de Cadenet (also near Trets); and Château Baron-Georges (near Puyloubier). There are co-ops in Trets, Rousset, Roquefort-la-Bedoule, Puyloubier and La Ciotat. The co-op de Mont-Ste-Victoire near Puyloubier, tel. 42-29-24-07, produces a lovely quality red and *rosé*.

8. **Vin de Pays de Bouches-du-Rhône** This is mainly *rosé*. Production is large — 15 million bottles. The quality is variable but inexpensive.

UK importers of Provence wines

The top-ranking wine importer specialising in the wines of Provence and the Rhône valley is Robin Yapp, Mere, Wiltshire, tel. (0747) 860423.

From a recent very informative catalogue I have noted the following châteaux of interest stocked by Robin Yapp.

- **Châteauneuf-du-Pape:** Domaine Font de Michelle; Domaine du Père Caboche; and Chante Cigale (by Christian Favier).

- **Gigondas:** Domaine du Grand Montmirail and Domaine St Gayan.

- **Vacqueyras:** produced by Pascal Frères.

- **Tavel:** La Forcadière.

- **Lirac:** La Fermade and a blanc de blanc by Armand Maby.

- **Beaumes-de-Venise:** Domaine de Durban and also Cave des Vignerons.

- **Côtes du Ventoux:** Vignerons de Beaumes-de-Venise.

- **Côtes du Rhône:** Co-op at Puymeras; Château du Rozay and Domaine St Gayan.

- **Côtes du Luberon::** Château de Canorgue; Mas du Peyroulet.

- **Bandol:** Mas de la Rouvière and Mont Caume.

- **Cassis:** Clos Sainte-Magdeleine.

- **Palette:** Château Simone.

- **Coteaux-des-Baux:** Domaine de Trévallon.

- **Coteau d'Aix:** Château de la Gaude.

- **Côtes de Provence:** Domaine des Hauts de St-Jean; Domaine des Feraud; and Domaine Richeaume.

The Oddbins chain stock Côtes du Rhône (Enclave des Papes from Valréas); Côtes du Rhône-Villages St Maurice; two Vacqueyras; a Gigondas (Domaine St Gayon); a Beaumes-de-Venise (from the Caves des Vignerons); and three Châteauneuf-du-Pape (Domaine Terres Blanches, Château Beaucastel and Château Fortia). There is also a Tavel *rosé* from the Caves des Vignerons. A good selection.

La Vigneronne, 105 Old Brompton Road, London SW7 3LE, tel. 01-589-6113, has several vintages of Château Vignelaure (Coteaux d'Aix-en-Provence); several Terres Blanches (Coteaux des Baux-de-Provence); many vintages of Château Simone (Palette); Château de Selle Rosé (Côtes de Provence); a Bandol *rouge* (Château de Varnières); as well as a Vacqueyras, Res du Paradis and many Châteauneuf-du-Pape.

Majestic Wine Warehouses also have a good selection from the region: four Côtes du Rhône; Jaboulet Ainés; Côtes de Ventoux; a Côtes du Rhône-Villages from Seguret; a Vinsobres Domaine du Moulin Vinson; a Lirac Domaine du Devoy; a Vacqueyras from Roger Combe; two Gigondas; a Châteauneuf-du-Pape (Château Mont Redon); and two Muscat de Beaumes-de-Venise (from the co-op and Jaboulet Ainé). They buy most of these wines through the shippers Mont Redon and Paul Jaboulet, as well as small quality growers such as Roger Combe, Denis Vinson and Devoy.

Christopher Piper Wines, 1 Silver Street, Ottery St Mary, Devon, EX11 1DB, tel. (0404) 814139, also have a good range including Côtes de Ventoux; Côtes de Luberon; several Côtes du Rhône Villages (Cairanne and Rasteau); a Lirac; a Vacqueyras; a Gigondas; a Rasteau *vin doux naturel;* a Tavel *rosé;* three Muscat de Beaumes-de-Venise; an Aix-en-Provence *rouge* (Domaines les Bastides); a Bandol; Châteauneuf-du-Pape and several Côtes de Provence.

The Wine Society, Gunnels Wood Road, Stevenage, Herts, SG1 2BG, tel. (0438) 741177, carries a good range. There are many Côtes du Rhône-Villages (Cairanne co-op, Vinsobres, Valréas, Rasteau and Vacqueyras); two Gigondas; six Châteauneuf-du-Pape (mainly Jaboulets les Cedres); a Lirac *blanc;* a Tavel *rosé* and a Muscat de Beaumes-de-Venise.

Which? Wine monthly magazine often carries out competitive 'blind' wine tastings by their panel of Masters of Wine. Recently they listed some of the Provençal (excluding Rhône) wines that they particularly liked:

- Domaine de Trevallon, Coteaux des Baux-en-Provence.

- Domaine les Bastides, Coteaux d'Aix-en-Provence, Jean Salen.

- Château Vignelaure, Coteaux d'Aix-en-Provence, Georges Brunel.

- Terres Blanches, Coteaux des Baux-en-Provence, Noel Michelin.

● Domaine des Paradis Blanc, Coteaux d'Aix-en-Provence

The supermarkets also stock some of these regional wines. Tesco has a *vins de pays* de Vaucluse, Cellier de St-Siffrein (near Carpentras) at a very competitive price. Sainsbury's have a Coteaux d'Aix-en-Provence in a winebox, and Marks and Spencer has a *vin de pays* des Bouches-du-Rhône (from Sica Rognets) with a ripe plummy nose and heaps of damson-like fruit.

Organic wines

These wines are made with the absolute minimum of chemicals and tend to cost a little more. One of the Provençal growers is Georges Dutel of Domaine Terres Blanches in Baux-en-Provence. There the hot sun produces fewer diseases than in wines grown in humid areas such as the Loire. Pierre Perrin, manager of the Château de Beaucastel in Châteauneuf-du-Pape, also uses organic methods. Oddbins sell his Côtes du Rhône Cru du Coudoulet. The Sainsbury chain sell the Domaine St Apollinaire Côtes du Rhône, quoted by a leading wine writer as 'spicy, peppery fruit, almost sweet in its richness with tannin and firmness'.

The wine tours of Provence

The C.I.V.C. 'Côtes du Rhône', 41 Cours Jean-Jaurès, Avignon, tel. 90-86-47-09 (who are very helpful particularly to members of the wine trade and wine writers!), have devised four regional wine tours. If you look closely enough they are signposted along the roads with *flèches*, or coloured arrows, to the 163 communes allowed the *appellation*.

● **La Route Rousse** (red colour) is 60 km long and starts at Bollène in the NW and straggles to Vaison-la-Romaine via Rochegude, Suze-la-Rousse (wine university), Bouchet, Ste-Cecile-les-Vignes, Tulette, Buisson, Villedieu and Vaison.

● **La Route Lavande** (lavender-lilac colour) is 70 km long, starts at Bollène and lurches towards Beaumes-de-Venise via Mondragon, Mornlas, Piolenc, Serignan-du-Comtat, Lagarde

137

Pareol, Ste-Cecile-les-Vignes, Cairanne, St Roman-de-Malegarde, south to Sablet, Gigondas, Vacqueyras and Beaumes-de-Venise.

● **La Route Orange** of 85 km starts appropriately at Orange and wobbles towards Nyons via Serignan-du-Comtat, Camaret-sur-Aigues, Travaillan, Rasteau, Roaix, north to Villedieu, west to Buisson, north to Visan, Richerenches, Grillon, Valréas, north again to Taulignan, east to Montbrison, Le Pegue, Rousset-les-Vignes, Novezan, St Pantaleon-les-Vignes, Venterol and wearily into Nyons.

● **La Route Dorée**, the golden route of 110 km from Avignon to Vaison, is not straightforward at all. Initially it goes to Le Poutel, south to Morières, Caumant-sur-Durance, north to Châteauneuf-de-Gadogne, Jonquerettes, St-Saturnie, Vedène, Entraigues (Sorgues if you can), Bedarrides and Châteauneuf-du-Pape. Then NE to Courthezon where you have a choice of east-flanking to Sarrians and Aubignon or north to Violes and east to Beaumes-de-Venise. Next north to Lafare, Suzette, Malaucène, Entrechaux, across the River Ouvèze to Fauçon, Puymeras and exhaustedly into Vaison-la-Romaine.

Remember that in each village mentioned there is a hospitable wine co-op, wine tasting caveaux, or private château who will help you with your tasting provided, naturally, that you buy a few bottles, preferably a case.

A Wine Club tour to Provence

The Wine Club, New Aquitaine House, Paddock Road, Reading, RG4 10Y, tel. (0734) 481713, offer a nine-day wine tour to Provence (usually early June) for about £840 based at good hotels in Aix and Avignon and visiting vineyards at Beaumes-de-Venise, Gigondas and Châteauneuf-du-Pape.

Hampton House Travel, tel. 01-549-2116, also arrange Provençal wine weeks based at Hôtel les Roches near Le Lavandou (40 km east of Toulon). The wines will be mainly Côtes de Provence in the eastern region.

Independent wine tours

Allez France, tel. (0903) 744279, has set up the Vinescapes department to provide a complete booking service for independent travellers to the French vineyards. All their selected hotels are working wine estates. Why not try them out on the Rhône Valley and Provence?

Some wine fêtes

The exact dates vary a little from year to year. In the valley of the Rhône leading into Provence they are taken very seriously. You would expect them all to be just after the vintage has been safely gathered, say in October. Not a bit of it, they appear at all times of the year.

Lauris (on D973 near Cadenet)	February - a Candlemas fair
Vinsobres (south of Valréas)	19/20 March — competition Côtes du Rhône-Villages
Châteauneuf-du-Pape	25 April — wine fête of St Mark
Baume-de-Transit (SW of Valréas)	23 May — wine competition
Taulignan (north of Valréas)	4/5 June — Fête des Vins
Monteux (near Carpentras)	5 June — Muscat grape fête
Violes (east of Orange)	July, 1st week — wine fair
Visan (SE of Valéas)	9 July - wine fair Confrèrie St Vincent
Vacqueyras (near Gigondas)	13/14 July — wine fair
Pertuis	14 July — wine fair
Gordes	14/15 July — Côtes du Ventoux wine fair
Buisson (NW of Vaison)	17 July — wine fair

Mondragon (SW of Bollène)	17 July — wine fair
Cairanne (west of Vaison)	24 July — wine fair
Mazan (near Carpentras)	24 & 30 July — Côtes du Ventoux wine fair
Saint Rémy	29–31 July — wine markets of Provence
Carpentras	End July — wine fair
Châteauneuf-du-Pape	August, 1st weekend — wine fair
Valréas	August, 1st Sunday — l'Enclave wine fair
Caromb (NE of Carpentras)	3/4 August — wine fair
Oppede (east of Cavaillon)	August, 1st Saturday — wine fair
Roaix (west of Visan)	7 August — Côtes du Rhône-Villages fête
Bedoin (NE of Carpentras)	7 August — Mont Ventoux wine fair
Beaumes-de-Venise	9 August — wine fair
Rasteau (west of Vaison)	14 August — evening wine festival
Rognes (west of Pertuis)	Mid August — wine fair
Seguret (SW of Vaison)	21 August — Provençal wine festival
Châteauneuf-du-Pape	September — vintage festival
Châteauneuf-de-Gadagne	September (beg) — vintage festival
Serignan-du-Comtat (NE of Orange)	13 September — vintage festival
Roaix (west of Visan)	October — vintage fête
Avignon	Mid-November — Côte du Rhône Primeur launch
Ste-Cecile-les-Vignes (west of Visan)	22 November — Musical Fête of *vin nouveau*
Vaison-la-Romaine	November, 3rd Sunday — Côte du Rhône Primeur

CHAPTER TWENTY-THREE:
CUISINE PROVENÇALE

Several delightful books have been written on this subject, for
instance by Elizabeth David, so all I need do is supply some
of the basics.

The flavours of Provence

Having lived and eaten well in France for many years, I have
little doubt that the Provençal style is more dramatic and
spicier than other regions. They have a wide range of local
herbs (basil, fennel, thyme, tarragon, rosemary, saffron, bay
leaves, sage, etc.) with which to ring the changes of flavouring. The ubiquitous garlic (sometimes raw onions), and the
availability of a wide range of locally grown vegetables
enhances every dish. Tomatoes, artichokes, red and green
peppers, asparagus, courgettes and aubergines make colourful
and tasty ingredients. On one market stall in Aix we counted
16 varieties of olives! Black olives are grown mainly around
Nyons, Salon and Carpentras and green ones near Nîmes, but
you will see olive trees everywhere and olive oil is usual in
most dishes. The curious black fungus, the valuable truffle, the
'black diamond', costs an astronomical £360 per kilo. To think
my wife and I once owned truffle oaks! The main truffle-
growing areas in Provence are Valréas, Carpentras, Apt and
Richerenches (NW of Visan). It is called *Tuber melanosporum*
and grows in light soil under oak trees, detected by specially-
trained dogs or pigs.

The Vaucluse is more rural and agricultural than the
Bouches-du-Rhône (which in turn has a wider range of fish).
In the huge market garden area around Carpentras and
Cavaillon, expect to see tomatoes, melons, limes and

strawberries at the former, and asparagus, melons and potatoes in the latter. The best almonds in France come from the southern Rhône valley in Provence, planted by the Romans in the fourth century.

Vaucluse specialities

Some of the Vaucluse specialities that you might expect to see on the menu are as follows:

● As *hors d'oeuvres* − *jambon cru de Malaucène; pâté de grives* (poor little thrushes); *saucisson de Sault* (with pepper-corns); asparagus from Lauris; *la caillette aux herbes* (quail in herbs); and *truffes sous la cendre* (Ventoux truffles).

● Next will be a river fish − trout, shad perhaps or crayfish *(écrevisses)* from the Sorgue, Auzon or Ouvèze, even *carpe farcie* (stuffed carp) or Rhône smoked eel *(catigau)*.

● Other specialities are *aioli* (garlic mayonnaise), *aubergine à la bohemienne* (egg plants), *tapenade* (cream of black olives and herbs crushed into a paste). There may be *omelette aux truffes* or various mushroom species called *grisets, cèpes* or *lactères du Ventoux*. If you are lucky you might find boar pâté *(sanglier)*, terrine laced with local marc or *le gratin de clovisses aux epinards* (clams with spinach).

● The main course could be *lièvre du Ventoux* (hare); *agneau des Monts du Vaucluse et du Valréas* (mountain lamb); *civet de porcelet à l'Avignonnaise* (pork stew); *coq au vin Châteauneuf-du-Pape* (chicken braised in a lovely wine); *la grillade des mariniers du Rhône* (traditional Rhône boatsmen's grilled beef); or *boeuf à l'estoufade*. Another speciality is duck or rabbit cooked in a dark aromatic gravy. Wretched little birds, such as lark, quail, pigeon or thrush, will appear on the menu.

● The French have a penchant for cake or *gâteaux*, perhaps *calissons* or *papalines d'Avignon*, *berlingot* sweets from Carpentras, nougat from Sault, crystallised fruits from Apt, or almond and cream *gâteau* called *caladons*, a concoction involving honey with a lavender flavour served with appropriate dessert wines — Muscat de Beaumes-de-Venise or Grenache de Rasteau.

Specialities south of Provence

Now let's have a look at the south of Provence. First of all comes the Camargue, where rice risotto with wild mushrooms is popular. The *gardiens* have a range of meat dishes, including *boeuf provençal, boeuf gardien* and bull stew. Small sand crabs called *tellines* are another Camargue delicacy. Sauces *à la provençale* always include tomato and garlic plus various herbs and spices.

On the coast you can find a wide range of *hors d'oeuvres* — anchovies, tuna, tomatoes, olives, mushrooms and various *crudités* (raw vegetables in a sauce). The southern *tapenade* which we first tried in Aix included anchovies, olives, capers and tuna pounded into a colourful paste — delicious! You may find *ratatouille* as well — a vegetable dish of tomatoes, aubergines, courgettes, green peppers, garlic and lots of olive oil.

Beside the Mediterranean, fish dishes dominate the culinary scene. Mullet, monkfish and sea bass are the best value, plus various shellfish, sea urchins *(oursins)*, clams, mussels and crab. Squid (which tastes to me like flavoured chicken), fresh sardines, *dourade* (John Dory), and bream (which is cooked with fennel) are to be found each morning in the fifty or so fish markets along the Provençal coast.

Marseille is the real home of *bouillabaisse*. For a large lunch party with adequate warning to the chef, as many as thirty to forty ingredients are included in the recipe. The various different fish and shellfish are cooked together in small pieces with a vegetable stock. Seasoning is then added — saffron, tomato, orange peel, thyme and bay leaves. A spicy sauce *(rouille)* of red pepper and garlic is added at the end.

Another popular dish is *bourride*, which has no shellfish or saffron but is based on white fish such as turbot, *dourade* and monkfish, with *aioli* sauce added. *Brandade de morue* is popular too, based on pounded salt cod mixed with olive oil, garlic and truffles. Other fish dishes you will encounter are red mullet *(rouget)*, sea bass *(loup de mer)* flamed with fennel or vine shoots, *moules marinières*, *oursins* (sea urchins), *violets* (sea squirts) and *clovisses* (clams).

If you are feeling brave enough, try another Marseille speciality called *pieds-paquets*, a mixture of sheep's trotters and tripe! The thrifty French will eat 100 per cent of any creature they kill — pig, sheep, rabbit or chicken — plus an appropriate sauce to take one's mind off what is *actually* being served! However, you cannot go wrong with the various *boeuf en daube* meat stewed in red wine and herbs, or lamb cassoulet perhaps with *pistou* (vegetable soup) to start with.

Cheeses in Provence lack variety. Banon and Cachat are the best if they have been marinated in wine or brandy with herbs. Local goat's cheese will be found in all the villages of Vaucluse, eaten either very young and creamy or vintage hard, but just as tasty!

Gastronomic tours of Provence

De Luxe Vacations, 53 Rue Grignan, 13006 Marseille, tel. 91-33-12-46, offer a three-day tour of Marseille and specific tuition by a chef in the art of preparing, and then eating, *bouillabaisse*. Then visit the Vieux Port and the Calanques to recover from the feasting. The same firm offers an alternative three- to four-day gastronomic holiday based on Sainte-Croix Abbey from 3,750–7,815 francs. Besides accommodation, full board and transport, there is a practical course in Provençal cuisine and gastronomic meals. Provence Voyages, 3 Bd. Raspail, 84000 Avignon, tel. 90-82-08-46, offer two Provençal cuisine tours, each from 2,500 francs, including full board and initiation by a grand chef!

Buying Provençal delicacies

For visitors wishing to purchase Provençal delicacies direct from the source, I have listed a few interesting ideas:

● **Olive oil** In the Bouches-du-Rhône there are eleven, and in the Vaucluse eight, co-operatives or *moulins* (crushing mills) and I am listing two in each department:

Perignon et Albert, Vallée des Baux, Rte des Fioles,

13430 Aureille; Moulin à Huile Co-operatif, Chemin du Mas Neuf, 13890 Mouries; Claude et Richard Mathieu, Rte du Moulin à Huile, 84580 Oppede. Soc. Co-op Agricole Oleiede, 'La Balméenne', 84190 Beames-de-Venise.

● **Cheese producers** Lucien Moutoux, 23 Chemin des Pachons, Ensues la Redonne (May-September). There are several goat farms in Entrechaux, Methamis (east of Carpentras), Monieux (SW of Sault).

● **Biscuits** Villaret from Nîmes.

● **Nougat** Sault.

● **Chocolate tartarinades** Tarascon.

● **Caramels berlingots** Carpentras, with *chiques* and *suce-miel* from Allauch.

● **Honey producers** Joseph Boudon, 63 Bd. National Lambesc (15 August–15 September). Miellerie des Butineuses, Rue de la Source, St Saturnin les Avignon, 84450.

● **Crystallised fruits** Melons from Avignon, various fruits from Apt.

● **Olive oil soap** Jacques Barle, Moulin à Huile, RN543 Surville Sud, Eguilles (not Sunday). Also look in Flassan (west of Sault), Vitrolles and Nyons.

● **Lavender** Several artisans in Aurel (north of Sault), Monieux, Sault, Valréas sell lavender flowers and essence.

● **Truffles** There are several small farmers in Blauvac (east of Carpentras), Entrechaux (near Vaison), Methamis, Richerenches (west of Valréas). In specialist shops try an unusual *terrine de chevreuil* (roe deer with thyme), *sanglier* (wild boar) or *perdix* (partridge). In a tin or jar it will make a most unusual present.

● **Wild boar farm** Visit Blauvac (east of Carpentras).

One last suggestion is to buy a bottle of Père Gauchère *frigolet*

145

— a blend of local brandy mixed with herbs of Provence, which is unobtainable outside the area.

Market days in the Vaucluse

To see the wide variety of fruits, vegetables, cheeses, wines and local delicacies available, the weekly market is much the best occasion. I list some of these held regularly in the leading towns.

Apt	Saturday
Avignon	Saturday mornings (Place Crillon, Place des Carmes)
Bollène	Monday
Carpentras	Friday
Cavaillon	Monday
Châteauneuf-du-Pape	Friday
Gordes	Tuesday
L'Isle-sur-la-Sorgue	Thursday and Sunday
Orange	Thursday
Pernes-les-Fontaines	Saturday
Pertuis	Friday
Sault	Wednesday
Sorgues	Sunday
Vaison-la-Romaine	Tuesday
Valréas	Wednesday
Visan	Friday

CHAPTER TWENTY-FOUR:
THE MAIN FESTIVALS AND EVENTS OF PROVENCE

Although I have tried to indicate when and where these take place in the context of writing about each town or large village, I believe a summary for the region may be of interest on a calendar basis.

Local fêtes

The majority of these events tend to take place in mid-summer. Indeed, every little village will have their annual *fête votive* (after the patron saint) usually in July or August. You will encounter descriptive words such as *manifestations, spectacles* or *animations*, but they tend to mean the same thing, i.e. a really good jolly! If you have a chance to book seats at a *repas champêtre,* this is a bucolic lunch (occasionally supper) lasting several hours, always out of doors, with many courses and lots of local wines *en pichet*, where you will meet several dozen strangers. By the end of the meal they will be lifelong friends. A *foire*, or fair, will be mildly commercial in the sense that, among the roundabouts and bumper-cars will be stalls selling local produce (pottery, leather, glass). The standard village fête will have a (not very good) band, with dancing *(un bal)* and probably a small travelling circus with sideshows, big wheel, slides, rifle shooting and some stands selling wine, honey, lavender, olive oil, soap etc. Some fêtes have specialities which are offered (often free) such as *soupe d'origin, aioli, cochons rôtis)* (at Allauch, *paella* (Arles), *oursins, anchoiade* (Cassis) and many more.

Each spring the medieval custom of Transhumance takes place, when huge herds of sheep or goats leave the hot grassless plains for the hillsides inland where vegetation survives better. The shepherds and their dogs lead their flocks off and return with them in late autumn. Two towns, Istres and St Rémy-de-Provence, celebrate the Transhumance in May and December when you will encounter 2,000 sheep roaming the streets!

Bull fighting

Whether you like it or not, most of southern Provence, and certainly Arles, Nîmes and the Camargue, is bullfighting country and has been for two thousand years. The Romans may have preferred gladiators beating each others' brains out, or wretched Christians being butchered, but the little black bulls featured in their amphitheatre revels are still to be seen.

There are two distinct styles of bullfighting. In Portugal, where I was brought up, all three parties (man, horse and bull) were treated with great respect. There was no grisly slaughter in the ring and the fighters displayed superb techniques, either on their magnificent horses or on their feet. The Spaniards take a different view. The horses are targets so that the bulls' ferocity can be tamed before the brave toreador will risk his life. In Provence, the traditional fighting is usually of the Portuguese school where no blood is shed, but the occasional Spanish fights take place and the advertising posters proudly proclaim 'to the death'.

The season starts at Easter and extends into autumn. Arenas are to be found in the main cities of Arles, Nîmes, Aix and Cavaillon. Rarely do you find bullfighting in the Vaucluse (Aubignan) but it can be found in many towns and villages in the Bouches-du-Rhône. These include Alleins, Barbentane, Boulbon, Cabanes, Châteaurenard, Cuges-les-Pins, Eguilles, Eyragues, Graveson, Istres, Lamanon, Maillane, Mas-Blanc-des-Alpilles, Méjanes, Miramas, Mouries, Noves, Peyrolles, Port St Louis, Pernes-les-Fontaines, Rognonas, St Andiol, St Chamas, St Etienne-du-Gré, St Rémy-de-Provence, Tarascon, Le Tholonet, and of course, Les Stes Maries-de-la-Mer.

The Provençal system is called *course à la cocarde*. Rash young men dressed in white, called *razeteurs*, endeavour to snatch (and then run like hell) a rosette called *cocarde* which has been previously attached to the bull's horns or round its head. The *razet* is a small metal hook held in the hand and used to pull the *cocarde* away from its temporary owner.

Bullfighting phrases

There are some key phrases attached to this sport.

● **Abrivado** is the arrival of the bulls and attendant *gardiens* on their white horses, with tridents, at the entrance of the village.

● **Bandido** is the moment when the bulls are encouraged to run wild through the streets thronged with spectators. The bulls may have *cocardes* attached for the lads in the crowd to snatch *en route* for the arena where the Course Camarguaise takes place.

● **Encierro** is a horseback game played by *gardiens* with a bull.

● **Ferrade** is the branding of the young bulls with the mark of its proprietor, and takes place at the bull farm.

● **Novillados** are courses by apprentice *toreros* or fighters.

● **Coup de Barrière** is the usually inelegant vault over the wooden barricade by the fleeing bullfighter. Often the bull follows too if he is nimble and has a full head of steam up. In this case the bullfighter seeks sanctuary in the ring!

● **Manades** back at the ranch *(mas)*, bulls, horses and sheep seem to mingle freely without apprehension. The cowboys keep the peace i.e. as *gardiens*.

● **Carreto ramado** is when the white horses are harnessed to traditional Saracen-style chariots (Charrette-de-St-Eloi) and take part in *défilés, corsos* or processions.

A calendar of Provençal events

January

St Andiol	Fêtes votive de la St Vincent	Dancing, concerts
Allauch	Fête de la St Clair on 6th	Folklore groups, five roasted pigs à la brioche
Sausset-les-Pins	Mois de l'oursin	Procession, tasting shellfish and wines
Aubignan	Grande Foire	On 2nd
Carpentras	Truffle markets, Friday a.m.	Place Aristide Briande
Richerenches	Truffle markets	Saturday a.m.
Bollène	Salon de Noël	Paintings, sculpture in Mairie
Seguret	Exhibition of Santons and crèches	
Visan	Wine fête, Confrèrie St Vincent	At Cave les Coteaux
Cassis	Pastorale Maurel	Provençal nativity

February

Avignon	Cheval Passion, horse events	Palais des Expositions
Carpentras/ Richerenches	Truffle markets	
Lauris	Artisanal fair of La Chandeleur	First Saturday
Vaison-la-Romaine	Asparagus markets	Tuesday a.m.
	Fair St Quenin	1st Tuesday after 15th
Carry-le-Rouet	Mois de l'oursin	Shellfish tasting, procession

Châteauneuf-les-Martigues	Carnival Castrum Vetus	Floats, processions, carnival
Coudoux	Corso Carnavalesque	Mardi Gras
Maillane	Fête votive la Ste Agathe	
Marseille	Fête des Notaires on 2nd	In Eglise des Pecheurs
Pelissane	Corso Carnivalesque	
Caderousse	Carnival on 13 February	Dancing in streets

March

Carpentras	Truffle markets	Friday a.m.
Mazan	Horse fair	On last Sunday
Mondragon	Fair	Tuesday after 10th
Richerenches	Truffle fairs	Saturday a.m.
Sorgues	Artisanal fair	Last weekend
Pelissane	Corso Fleuri	End of month
Orange	Carnival	26/27th

April

Valréas	Lamb and Easter fair	
Sault	Easter Monday *grande foire*	
Arles	*Cocardes* and *corridas*/Fête des Gardiens	Provence bullfights
Eyguières	Fête of le St Marc	Folklore festival of La Crau
Martigues	Spring fête	In 2nd week
Meyreuil	Fête of le St Marc	On 25th
Les Stes Maries-de-la-Mer	Abrivado, Bandido	Bull course *à la cocardes*

151

May

Caderousse	Fête du Muguet (lily-of-the-valley)	
Orange	Spring Fair	27-30th
Bedarrides	Ascension horse fair	
Grillon	Lamb and asparagus fairs 28/29th	Place Bourgade
Les Taillades	*Grande Foire*	29th
Mormoiren	Asparagus fair	12th
Pertuis	*Grande Foire*	
Arles	*Cocardes* and *corridas*/Fête des Gardiens	Provence bullfights
Barbentane	Horse fair	2nd Sunday
Châteaurenard	Horse fair	2nd Sunday
Lambesc	Corso Fleurs	2nd/3rd Sunday, procession with flowers
Peypin	Fête votive on 25th	Dances, processions
Port-St-Louis-du-Rhône	Fête sans Frontière	End of month Dances, processions
Rognonas	Fête du Bon Ange	Beginning
St Rémy-de-Provence	Charette des Anes	Folklore, dances, torch processions
	Fête de la Transhumance	2,000 sheep and goats in streets
Les Stes Maries-de-la-Mer	Journée Baroncellienne	26th Folklore dances
Salin-de-Giraud	Concours de Farandoles	Provençal costume dances
Salon-de-Provence	Fête des Bressons Blazets	*Aioli*, fun and games

Le Tholonet	Fête votive de la Ste-Croix	1st Sunday Cavalcades, bullfights
Le Thor	Fête de la Colline de Thouzon	1st Sunday Folklore fête
Mazan	Fête du Carri on 1 May	Peasant becomes lord of the manor
Malemort-du-Comtat	Fête du Muguet on 1 May	Provençal song and dances
Methamis	Fête of la Chapele Ste-Foy	Pentecost Monday fête
Mondragon	Fête du Drac	
Monteux-le-Beaucet	Pilgrimage of St Gens	3rd Sunday
Roussillon	Ascension festival d'Ocre and Colour	

June

Camaret	Fête votive on 1st	
Violes	Spring Fair	11–13th
	Fishermen	18th
Piolenc	Fête votive	25–27th
Jonquieres	Grande Foire	1st Sunday
Malaucene	Grande Foire	1st Sunday
Menerbes	Dog fair	12th
	Horse fair	19th

Barbentane, Les-Baux-de Provence, Cabannes, La Ciotat, Cavaillon, Eygalières, Eyguières, Fontvieille, Istres, Mallemort, Martigues, Miramas, La Roque d'Antheron, Roquefort-la-Bedoule, Roquevaire, St-Cannat, Trets, Valréas, Sault, Allauch and Aubagne all celebrate the Feast of St Jean on 23 or 24 June with folklore, processions, fireworks, prehistoric monsters etc. The feast of St Peter of 29 June is celebrated in Martigues and La Ciotat but in July at Auriol, Molleges, Peynier.

Cassis	Fête de la Mer, 1st week	Folklore, anchoiade
Boulbon	Fête des Vendanges on 1st	The bottles are blessed
Venelles	Fête patronale of St Hyppolite	
Tarascon	Fête du Cordage	11–14th
	Fête of la Tarasque last Sunday	*Major event!*
Salon de Provence	Fête des Canourgues Fête des Aires de la Dine	
Salin-de-Giraud	Folklore fête in arena	1st Sunday
	Fêtes Champetres, last Sunday	Fireworks, folklore
Les Stes-Maries-de-la-Mer	Grande Fête votive – mid June	*Major event!*
St Rémy-de-Provence	Musical fête, end of month	Folklore, ferrade
St-Chamas	Harbour fête, 3rd Sunday	Jousting, fireworks
Rognac	Fête des Barjaquets on 1st	
Port-St-Louis-du-Rhône	Fête du Faubourg Hardon	
Molleges	Fête of St Eloi	Folklore 'Carreto Ramado'
Marseille	Festival du Quartier	Folklore, concerts, dances
Sorgues	International festival of jazz	End of month
Fos-sur-Mer	Fête des Carabins	3rd week
Bollène	Fête du Papagai	Last Saturday

July

Avignon	Grand Festival and Artisan fair in Allées de l'Oulle	*Major event*
Gigondas	Fête votive	16–19th
Serignan	Soirée des Campions	13th
Violes	Fête votive, wine fête	2nd, 3rd and 5th
L'Isle-sur-la-Sorgue	Provençal market and festival	End of month
Gordes	Horse fair on 14th	Place de la Poste
Apt	Treteaux de Nuit	End of month
Bollène	Festival	
Cavillon	Folklore Fridays Bullfighting Saturdays	
Valréas	Theatrical evenings de l'Enclave	
Vaison-la-Romaine	Festival and 'les Choralies'	International song concert
Sorgues	Folklore festival	2nd weekend
Seguret	*Crèches* and *santons* exhibition	
Orange	Choregies	*Major event*
Aix-en-Provence	Semano Prouvencalo	Songs, poetry, music, theatre
	La Saison d'Aix	*Major event*
Arles	Cocarde d'Or, 1st week	Course Camarguaise
Aubagne	Folklore festival, 1st week	'Li Dansaire de Garlabau
Château-Gombert	St Eloi fête, international folklore festival	Processions, dances
La Ciotat	Harbour fête on 9th Provençal fête	Venetian fête, fireworks

Fontvieille	Provençal dances at Daudets Mill	22nd
Fos-sur-Mer	Fête de la Mer, middle of month	Water jousting etc.
Graveson	Fête of St Eloi, last Sunday	Provençal dances, courses
Istres	Fête de Rassuen, 3rd Sunday	Courses
Maillane	Fête of St Eloi	'Carreto Ramado', Courses
Martigues	Fête Venitienne, 1st Saturday	Fireworks, processions
Méjanes	Feria du Cheval, 11–14th	Horseriding in arenas
Noves	Fête locale on 14th	'Pegoulado' ball, Courses
St Rémy-de-Provence	Grande Fête on 14th	Abrivado, Courses, fireworks
	Marché de Provence, last weekend	Wine and food fair
Les Stes Maries-de-la-Mer	Fête Virginienco, 3rd Sunday	Young girls in Arlesien finery
Salon-de-Provence	Fête de Bel Air, 1st weekend	
	Fête locale, 2nd weekend	Torchlight procession
Trets	Fêtes of St Eloi, St Christophe weekend after 14th	Grand Corso with 100 horsemen
Nyons	Olive oil and folklore festival	1st fortnight

August

Allauch	Fête du Logis-Neuf, mid-month	Folklore procession

Alleins	Fête of St Pierre es Lien	Abrivado courses
Auriol	Fête votive, beginning of month	Three days
La Barben	Fête votive, 1st week	Three days
Barbeatane	Fête votive, last Sunday	Courses, folklore dances
Boulbon	Fête St Eloi, last weekend	'Carreto Ramado'
Carry-le-Rouet	Fête votive, 15th	Fireworks, folklore, procession
Châteaurenard	Fête Ste-Madelaine	Enciero, aioli, courses
La Ciotat	Fete du Quartier Fontsainte	1st Weekend
Cuges-les-Pins	Fête St Eloi — 5 days	Cavalcade, courses
Eygalières	Fête votive St Laurent	1st Sunday, 3 days
Eyguières	Fête votive St Vérédeme	Courses, processions, ferrade
Eyragues	Fête St Symphorien	Last Sunday, 3 days
Fontvieille	Fête votive St Pierre es Lien	Manades contest, procession
Fos-sur-Mer	Fête locale, 10–15th	Balls, 'animations'
Istres	Fête St Etienne, beginning month	Corridas, jousts, regattas, folklore, dances, *aioli*
Lambesc	Fête votive St Janvier, last Sunday	Fireworks, repas champêtre
Lascours	Fête St Eloi, last Sunday	Fireworks, dances, processions

Marseille	Fête St Pierre, beginning month	Jousts at l'estaque harbour
Mas Blanc des Alpilles	Fête votive, 13–17th	Procession, courses, *aioli*
Miramas	Fête St Jean, last Sunday	Fireworks, balls, four days
Port St Louis du Rhône	Faubourg fêtes	Courses, dances,
Rognonas	Fête St Roch, 3rd Sunday	'Animations,
Roqueraire	Fête St Eloi, 15th	'Carreto Ramado', fireworks, galas
Les Stes Maries-de-la-Mer	Feria Saintoise 14–17th	Corridas, courses, ball, fireworks, the lot!
Sausset-les-Pins	Fête Venitienne	Fireworks, floats, ball
Senas	Fête votive, last week	Donkey races, fireworks, ball etc.
Trets	Fête St Barthelemy, 24th	'Animations'
Velaux	Fête St Eloi, 1st week	Corso, floats, ball, animations
Orange	Fête St Barthelemy, 26–29th Grand Fair on 15th	
Piolenc	Fête de l'ail (garlic) and wine	27–28th
Serignan	La Grappe d'Or, 5–10th	Medieval event in open
Avignon	Foire artisanale/jousting, 15th	In Allées de l'Oulle

Châteauneuf-du-Pape	Medieval artisanal fair	1st weekend
Lacoste	Foire artisanale	Last Sunday
Merindol	Pottery fair	15–16th
Pertuis	Grande foire	15th
Sault	Grande foire	16th
Valréas	Grande foire St Dominique	1st Sunday
Apt	Treteaux de Nuit	
Bedoin	Medieval contest Tir Armes	Including archery
	Walking contest over Mt Ventoux	Last Sunday
Cavaillon	Folklore Fridays of Cavaillon Courses on Saturdays	
Gordes	Festival — *spectacle equestre*	15th
La Tour d'Aigues	Festival in château	
Malaucène	Summer fête, walking contest Farigoule	Third weekend
Pernes-les-Fontaines	Courses and song contests	
Piolenc	Garlic festival, end month	
Seguret	Provençal festival, 3rd Sunday	Theatre and folklore
Vaison-la-Romaine	Festival — les Choralies	
Valréas	Les Nuits theatricales of l'Enclave	
Venasque	Traditional fête, artisanal exhibition	

September

Aix-en-Provence	Anniversary birth Frédéric Mistral	Gathering of Félibres Provençal folklore
Arles	Fêtes des Premines du Riz	10 day festival, jousts
Aubagne	Fête de la Paix	Corso, concerts, aioli, concerts
Auriol	Fête des Vendanges (vintage wine)	1st weekend
Cassis	Fête des Vins de Cassis beginning	Tasting, procession, folklore
Chateaurenard	Fête of St Omer	Courses, charettes, floats
Graveson	Fête votive	Courses, enciero, aioli
Mallemort	Fête St Michel	Provençal dances, procession
Mouries	Fête des Olives Vertes	Abrivado, Pegoulade, Courses
Noves	Fête of St Eloi, 2 days	'Carreto Ramade', processions
Pelissane	Fête votive St Maurice, 2nd Sunday	Wine fair, courses aioli
Puyloubier	Fête of St Eloi	Hare races, aioli, 'aubade'
Le Puy-Ste-Reparade	Fête of St Michel	Fireworks, folklore, processions
St Chamas	Fête of St Leger, 1st Sunday	Abrivado, enciero, aioli etc.

St Remy-de-Provence	Fête votive, 4th Sunday	Concerts, dances, courses, 'abrivado'
Salon-de-Provence	Fête du Jumelage (twinned town)	Folklore, procession
Villelaure	Artichoke and horse fair	Last weekend
Courthezon	Artisanal fair	1st weekend
Caderousse	Fête votive of St Michel	
Bollène	Provence fête	
Cavaillon	Traditional fête of St Gilles	1st Monday
Villelaure	Artichoke fair	Last weekend

October

La Bouilladisse	Fête aux Vins	'Animations'
La Destrousse	Vins de Provence Foire	Also horse and dog fairs
Jouques	Fête votive of St Batie	Folklore, dances
Mallemort	Journée Provençale	Onion soup, aioli, dancing
Caderousse	Fête of Ste Michelle	

November

Avignon	Festival de Jeux de l'Esprit	Very unusual, tarot and belot cards etc.
	Baptism, Côtes du Rhône Primeur (young wines)	
Vauvenargues	Grande Fête of St Hubert	Cavaliers, hunting processions
Stes Maries-de-la-Mer	Commemorative ceremony	'Abrivado', bandio dances

December

Istres	Fête des Bergers, 2nd weekend	2,000 sheep in streets, processsion gardiens
Château-Gombert	Pastorale Maurel	
Marseille	Pastorale Maurel	
Martigues	Vieillee Calendale	Song and dances
Tarascon	Marché aux Santons, 1st weekend	In Cloister of Cordeliers
Caderousse	Reveillon of St Sylvestre	
Carpentras	Truffle markets every Friday a.m.	
	Santon exhibition	In Caveau des Vins
Apt and Aubignon	Fair of Ste Luce, 13th	
Apt	Salon des Santonniers	
Valréas	Foire des Gourmands	Saturday before Christmas
	Provençal Christmas crèche	
Gordes	Artisanal exhibition	In Tourist Office

When you arrive in Provence, ask immediately at the Tourist Office for the exact date and place of the next *manifestation*. The *corsos* or *defilés* (processions) and *carnavalesques* are the most exciting – usually at Pentecost – and some have a theme. L'Isle-sur-la-Sorgue has a *corso nautique* on the river and canals; in Valréas there is a theme of lavender; in Villes-sur-Auzon it is for children *(enfantin)*. An *aubade* is a town concert; a *bal* may not be a sophisticated ball and the music may be dated, but it will be fun! The *Félibres* are the folklore groups with song, dance and traditional costume. *Feux d'artifices* are fireworks. The *Garanaudo*, or *Tauresque*, is a medieval monster, mobile and a blend of comedy and tragedy. A *Pegoulado* is a folklore procession with lit torches *(flambeaux)*. *Tournoi de joutes* is a competition for young men in, on or over water, jousting with long poles.

CHAPTER TWENTY FIVE: CAMP SITES

Many visitors to Provence with kids in tow will choose a week or more at a camp site, not only for reasons of economy but also because of the wide range of outdoor opportunities for amusement (for everyone!).

Current prices per head per day inclusive of most charges relate to the site facilities available, or situation.

4 stars 35–55 francs   (145 per day 4 people)
3 stars 30–50 francs   (85–105 per day 4 people)
2 stars 25-45 francs   (45 per day 2 people)
1 star 20–40 francs   (40–63 per day 3 people)

There are 92 sites in the Vaucluse and 90 in the Bouches-du-Rhône. Space does not permit them to be listed but if you write to either of these two addresses asking for their *dépliant campings*, you should receive all the information you need to know.

(a) Chambre Départementale de Tourisme de Vaucluse, la Balance, Place Campana, B.P. 147, 84008 Avignon, or tel. 90-86-43-42.

(b) Comité Départementale du Tourisme des Bouches-du-Rhône, 6 Rue du Jeune-Anacharsis, 13001 Marseille, or tel. 91-54-92-66.

The most popular places are Avignon (6), Arles (6), La Ciotat (7), Martigues (11), St Mitre-les-Remparts (4). I have listed the largest camp sites for really gregarious readers.

Vaucluse
Avignon (1,080 and 900), Aubignan (600), Bedoin (500),
Cavaillon (600), Gordes (600), La Isle-sur-la-Sorgue (600),
Lourmarin (600), Pertuis (800), St Marcellin-les-Vaison (600),
St Saturnin d'Apt (600), Vaison-la-Romaine (1,000).

Bouches-du-Rhône
Carry-le-Rouet (700), La Ciotat (533), Martigues (400), Les
Stes Maries-de-la-Mer (2,200). The Domaine de Belezy at
Bedoin is a nudist camping site over 25 hectares.
    A useful checklist of amenities on offer is shown below.

Douches chaudes/froides	Hot or cold showers available
Eau	Water laid on for individual caravans
Electricité, branchment	Individual points for caravans
Laverie	Laundry facilities
Locations	Whether mobile homes, caravans, tents are available to rent
Gardiennage	Day and night campsite guarded
Commerces	Shop(s) on site
Garderie d'enfants	Day nursery
Animaux acceptées/pas acceptées/libre	Pets allowed/not allowed/ free
Aire de jeux	Playing area for children
Television	Television available
Piscine	Swimming pool
Baignade	Bathing in pond, lake, river or sea
Equitation	Horse-riding facilities
Tennis	Tennis
Location vélo	Bicycle renting
Animation	Entertainment in the camp site

| **Langues** | Languages spoken; GB = English |
| **Restaurant/Bar/Plats Cuisines** | Eating facilities for various types of food |

Usually you will get a helpful *situation géographique* such as:

C = Campagne (countryside)
M = Montagne (hills)
L = Lac/plan d'eau (lake)
R = Rivière (river for canoe or swimming)
F = Forêt (wooded)
O = Borde de mer ou plage (near sea or beach)
V = Village (in or near village)

CHAPTER TWENTY SIX:
FUN AND GAMES IN PROVENCE

Water Sports

Marinas

There are a number of marinas along the shoreline of 'Provence on Sea'. I have coded the harbours 'M' for Marina and 'BR' for boat rental.

Arles (M); Berre l'Etang (M); Carry-le-Rouet (M, BR); Cassis (M, BR); La Ciotat (M, BR); Ensuès la Redonne (M); Fos-sur-Mer (M); Marignane (M); Marseille (M, BR); Martigues (M); Port-de-Bouc (M); Port St-Louis-du-Rhône (M); St Chamas (M); Stes Maries-de-la-Mer (M, BR); and Sausset-les-Pins (M, BR).

Jousting matches

During the high season at Cassis, La Ciotat, Fos-sur-Mer, Martigues, Sausset-les-Pins, Miramas and Les Stes Maries-de-la-Mer. Traditional pole fighting from boats by *matelots*.

Water parks

Aquacity is an aquatic park in Plande Campagne with its own restaurant and bar, tel 91-96-12-13. Frioul Islands Maritime Park is a sailing and boat cruising centre offshore. Access is by boat from Marseille Vieux Port.

Fishing

The European Fishing Championships, the Moulinet d'Or, is for big fish weighing over 200 kilos! The Vaucluse department is best for river fishing, particularly at Apt, Beaumes-de-Venise, Carpentras, Châteauneuf-du-Pape, Fontaine-de-Vaucluse, L'Isle-sur-la-Sorgue, Pernes-les-Fontaines, Velleron and Pertuis. Ask at the Tourist Office for a temporary permit for which you will have to pay a small fee.

Spa and thermal baths
Camoins Hydropathic Estat, Marseille, tel. 91-43-02-50.
Thermal Baths, 55 Cours Sextius, Aix-en-Provence, tel. 42-26-01-18.
N.D. de Bon Voyage, Ave. Frédéric Mistral, La Ciotat, tel. 42-83-90-20.
Le Grand Large, 42 Ave. du Grande Large, Marseille, tel. 91-73-25-88.
Thalassotherapy Centre, 96 Promenade de la Corniche Kennedy, Marseille, tel. 91-52-01-03.

Canoeing/kayaks
These can be hired at several places in the Vaucluse on the River Durance and tributaries and at Fontaines-de-Vaucluse, L'Isle-sur-la-Sorgue. Ask for details from the Tourist Office.

Caving/pot holing

This is known as *spéléologie*. It is found mainly in the Vaucluse at L'Isle-sur-la-Sorgue, Mirabeau, Sault, Fontaine-de-Vaucluse, Cavaillon (Tourist Office) and on guided visits to Le Thor.

Rock/hill climbing

Clubs can be found at Aubagne, Aurons, Cassis, Châteauneuf-les-Martigues, Ensuès-la-Redonne, Marseille (Tourist Office), Le Tholonet, St Chamas, St Antonin and Puyloubier. In the Vaucluse there is climbing at Gigondas (Les Dentelles), Le Thor, Mirabeau, and villages on the slopes of Mont Ventoux, Buoux.

Ski-ing

This takes place mainly in the Vaucluse at Bedoin, Carpentras, Malaucène, Mirabeau — on Mont Ventoux, of course, Mont Serein and Sault.

Walks/hiking

Most Tourist Offices in the Vaucluse will give you advice on local walks, clubs and Grandes Randonnées in the region. Malaucène has organised walks on Mont Ventoux range, and Sault and Vacqueyras have walks on Les Dentelles de Montmirail, also at Vaison-la-Romaine. A.D.T.R., La Lauze, Route de la Nesque, 84570 Par Mormoiron, tel. 90-61-83-23, offers a wide range of organised walks in the Ventoux and Luberon ranges.

Hang-gliding

Avignon Tourist Office has details of local clubs.

Hunting

Ask at the Tourist Office at Apt, Cabrières d'Aigues and Violes for details.

Archery

Avignon Tourist Office has details of local clubs.

Flying clubs

There are clubs in the Bouches-du-Rhône at Eyguières, Istres, St Rémy-de-Provence, Salon-de-Provence, Sausset-les-Pins, Trets and Vitrolles. In the Vaucluse, clubs are at Violes, Visan and Pernes-les-Fontaines.

Cycle rentals

Bicycles are available in Tarascon, Salon-de-Provence, St Rémy-de-Provence, Les Stes Maries-de-la-Mer, La Roque d'Antheron, Marseille, Istres, La Ciotat, Carry-le-Rouet, Aubagne and Arles.

Tennis

Every town and village has hard courts and local clubs.

Motorcycle rough riding

Spring competitions take place at Pernes-les-Fontaines, Lagarde Paréol and Ste Cecile-les-Vignes.

Rifle range shooting

You can shoot at Bedoin and Valréas in the Vaucluse.

Dolmen spotting

There is a dolmen at Menerbes, the only one in the Vaucluse.

Holiday villages

These are ideal for families with children — try Istres, Carry-le-Rouet, Carnoux-en-Provence, Arles, La Roque d'Antheron, Roquefort-la-Bedoule and St Rémy-de-Provence.

Wild West villages

There is the OK Corral at Cuges-les-Pins, tel. 42-73-80-05 (March–October) and Eldorado City at Ensuès-la-Redonne, tel. 42-79-86-90.

Golf clubs

Les Milles, Cobriès, Allauch, Fureau, La Valentine and Bouc Bel Air all have golf clubs. They are also at Mallemort and Salon-de-Provence.

Golfing holidays

Two- or three-day golfing holidays in Provence can be reserved through the following firms:

- Résidence les Citadines, Jas de Bouffran, 13090 Aix-en-Provence, tel. 42-20-65-72. A three-day holiday including free (!) tuition at the Aix golf club and half-board costs about 1,500–1,980 francs.
- A.T.M. Voyages, 15 Place Castil-Blaze, 84302 Cavaillon, tel. 90-71-37-66, offer a two-day golfing holiday at Châteaublanc course near Avignon. Accommodation, car hire and green fees included, cost 2,320–3,785 francs.

● Le Mas des Amandiers, Route d'Avignon, 13690 Graveson, offer golf on four different courses (Nîmes, Les Baux, Servannes, Châteaublanc or Grand Avignon from 1,000 francs for 3 days).

Indoor sport – casinos!

You can find casinos at Aix-en-Provence, Carry-le-Rouet, Cassis and La Ciotat.

Horse racing events

Head for Avignon (Ascension and Pentecost meetings), Cavaillon (May and September), Carpentras (Easter and July), Sault (August), Bollène (June) and L'Isle-sur-la-Sorgue (August).

Horse riding in Provence

Since the white horses of the Camargue symbolise part of the charm of Provence, I have included a summary of the *centres équestres* from whom the visitor can hire horses or join riding schools.

Bouches-du-Rhône (E = English spoken)			Tel.
Aix	Club Hippique, Chemin des Cavaliers	(E)	42-59-02-56
Aix	Le Centaure, Les Pinchinats	(E)	42-23-59-85
Aix	Beaurecueil, Les Terres Rouges		42-28-90-02
Allauch	Campagne la Louise, La Pounche		91-68-07-38
Arles	Domaine de l'Estajan, Mas Véran-Qtr. Fourchon	(E)	90-93-23-52
Aubagne	Route de Gemenos		42-82-33-79
Les Baux	Club Hippique de Carita		90-97-44-26
Istres	Les Heures Claires	(E)	42-56-10-87
Mallemort	Domaine du Vergon		90-59-12-57
Marseille	33 Traverse de Carthage	(E)	91-73-72-94
Port de Bouc	Domaine de Castillon		42-41-19-53

Salon-de-Provence	Chemin de Bastidettes, Rte d'Eyguières		90-43-96-85
Saint-Cannat	Les Décanis		–
Tarascon	Quartier de Lansac		90-91-42-87
Tarascon	Mas de Longalène	(E)	–
Vitrolles	Les Collets Rouges		42-89-29-93

Vaucluse

Apt	Relais de Roquefure	(E)	90-74-22-80
Apt	Cheval en Luberon, Qtr de Roquefure	(E)	90-74-64-83
Avignon	La Barthelasse, Chemin du Mt Blanc	(E)	90-85-83-48
Bedoin	Pierravon		90-65-61-10
Bedoin	Le Meneque	(E)	90-65-66-39
Bonnieux	Randonnées du Luberon, Col Pointu	(E)	90-74-40-48
Camaret	La Rigole		90-37-27-44
Carpentras	Saint Ponchon	(E)	90-60-08-40
Castellet	Camp des Bardons		90-75-20-87
Caumont	Chemin des Jourdans		90-22-26-56
Cheval Blanc	Camping des Genets		90-78-36-87
Courthezon	La Ribousse	(E)	90-70-88-42
Cucuron	La Rasparine		90-77-21-46
Entraigues	Ranch de l'Etalon Blanc	(E)	90-83-16-26
Gordes	des Luquets	(E)	90-72-07-97
Goult	Mas de la Barbe		90-72-32-76
Grillon	Ferme Saint Martin		90-35-06-75
Joucas	Mas du Buis	(E)	90-72-02-22
Lagarde d'Apt	Ferme les Esfourgniaux		90-75-01-04
Le Pontet	La Gourmette, Route de Védène		90-31-04-91
Les Taillades	Ranch El Dorado		90-71-03-04
L'Isle sur la Sorgue	La Catherine, Chemin du Lagnien	(E)	90-38-16-13
Malaucène	Les 3 Rivières		90-36-18-79
Mazan	Manade du Jonquier, Route de Sault		90-69-84-76
Mormoiron	Hautes Briguières	(E)	90-61-93-55

Oppede	La Bastide, Qtr St-Antonin	(E)	90-71-87-56
Orange	ler R.E.C., Route du Parc		90-51-63-85
Piolenc	L'Eperon, 'la Deronne'		90-51-59-24
Roussillon	Le Trefle à 5 feuilles, les Madons	(E)	90-75-63-90
St Martin-de-la-Brasque	Hatas de la Brasque	(E)	90-77-62-60
Sannes	Roque Colombe	(E)	90-77-65-08

Some *centres équestres* are more sophisticated than others, with swimming pools, archery, tennis and horse-ball as well as polo! Fees vary, of course. For an hour's riding or lesson a pony could cost 30–60 francs, and a horse 50–70 francs. But a day's riding could cost 150–250 francs. Meals are often available for 50 francs per person.

There are also many *gîtes équestres* where you and your newly acquired equine friend can put up for the night. *Nourriture* for the latter is 20–30 francs, bed for you is a mere 35–50 francs. One place charges 120 francs for dinner, bed and breakfast for you and your friend combined!

Some useful addresses

- Association Département du Tourisme Equestre (Vaucluse), C.D.T., Place Campana, B.P. 147, 84008 Avignon, tel. 90-25-38-91.

- Comité Département des Sentiers de Grandes Randonnées (walks), Les Fontaines-du-Levant, 63 Ave. César-Franck, 840000 Avignon. (Note that Robertson McCarton Limited, 122 Kings Cross Road, London WC1, have published walks in Provence with detailed maps and G.R. itineraries.)

- Fédération Département de Pêche (fishing), 5 Bd. Champfleury, 84000 Avignon, tel. 90-86-62-68.

- Fédération Département de Chasse (hunting), 64 Rue Thiers, 84000 Avignon, tel. 90-82-51-99.

- Fédération Département de la Montagne et Club Alpin (Ski-ing), 7 Rue St-Michel, 84000 Avignon, tel. 90-38-14-67.

173

- Transhumance, Clos de la Cristole, 84140 Monfavet, tel. 90-95-57-81.

- Sport and Montagne, 50 Rue Carnot, Avignon, tel. 90-85-61-45 offer a wide range of climbing, walking, mountain-bikes, orienteering, *cuisine du terroir* and ornithological tours and courses. As does Michel Barban, 32 Place des Cafés, 84450 St Saturnin les Avignon.

- An alpine and ski instructor with programmes in the Dentelles de Montmirail is André Charmetant, 56 Ave. Paul de Vivie, 84210 Pernes-les-Fontaine, tel. 90-66-50-28.

CHAPTER TWENTY SEVEN:
BUYING PROPERTY IN PROVENCE

Owning a cottage in Provence must rank as being one of life's most attractive pipedreams. Despite the distance and the cold winter mistral winds, more and more British are buying houses in Provence either as *maisons secondaires* or for a more permanent home, on retirement.

This chapter lists some of the possibilities. My advice is to spend a few weeks touring around — out of season. If you plan to live there more or less permanently (and our friendly Inland Revenue allows you an average of three months a year back in the UK), then try to visit Provence at its very worst so that you realise it is not a land of milk and honey, Châteauneuf-du-Pape and constant sunshine!

Estate agents

Several UK estate agents have close links with their opposite numbers in Provence. They share the rather generous agency commission allowed in France, charged on top of the seller's price. The advantage is that you can have extra and free professional advice about the legal pitfalls (i.e. your children will automatically have the right to equal shares in your French property on your death).

- Rutherfords, 7 Chelsea Manor Street, London, SW3 3TW, tel. 01-351-4454, always have a number of Provençal properties on their books. Other possibilities include:
- French Elite, tel. 01-994-2721.
- Ryder International, tel. (0425) 277178/779333.
- Barton Cook & Sams, tel. (0602) 582526.

- Provence Properties, 33 Station Road, Barton under Needwood, Staffs, DE13 8DR, tel. (0283) 712205.
- France Mediterranée, tel. 01-645-0773.
- France Immobilier, tel. 01-481-0521.
- In one of my favourite towns of Vaision-la-Romaine, Alpha Agence Immobilière, Ave. Jules Ferry has properties from 290,000 francs.
- In Pertuis try Sainclair, 295 Cours de la République; in Apt, Agence M. Parfait (O.R.P.I.), 52 Ave. Victor Hugo, tel. 90-74-23-90; in Orange, Agence Silvy, 44 Cours. A. Briand.
- In Aix there are no less than thirty Agences Immobilières, including many on the Cours Mirabeau (Thermes at No. 10, Sud Gestion at No. 61, Sud Est at No. 53, Provence Immobilière at No. 28, Mirabeau at No. 11, I.P.A. at No. 55, du Centre at No. 3). SAFRU, 16 Place Albert ler, Uzès, 30700 have apartments for sale near Avignon's Papal Palace.
- Further south on the Mediterranean there are several agents in Cassis (Agence du Port, Rue de l'Arène) for coastal properties. In La Ciotat, try Cassis Agence, 49 Ave. Victor Hugo, tel. 42-01-35-06 or Les Maisons de Cassis, 7 Rue A. Rossat, tel. 42-01-76-81.
- La Tour d'Aigues (pop. 2,000) is an attractive little town on the slopes of the Luberon hills, NE of Pertuis. Two estate agents there are Luberon Immobilier, tel. 90-77-52-12 and Agence Sud Luberon, tel. 90-77-41-64.
- For a list of estate agents in and around Nîmes, write to Chambre des Agents Immobilières, 11 Rue Racine, tel. 66-21-72-58.
- One of the best agents in Avignon is Avignon-Provence Immobilier, 30 Rue Grande Fusterie, tel. 90-85-90-95.

Other important addresses

- French mortgages can be arranged through Charles Hamer Financial Services, tel. 01-579-2731. John Garner, tel. 01-546-9080, or the French Property Investment Centre, tel. (0628) 777478.

- Legal services and advice are offered by the solicitors Henry C. F. Fowkes, Susannah Wesley House, Stothard Place, Bishopsgate, London EC2M 4RP, tel. 01-247-0636.
- For removals to France try Corfield Limited, tel. (0425) 621172 or Removals France, tel. (0304) 614294.
- Structural surveys in France can be arranged through Chartered Surveyors — try Raymond Harman Associates, tel. (0797) 21682 or Adrian Barrett, tel. (0722) 333583.
- Renovation or management of French properties can be arranged through LMC Property Company of Ashford, tel. (0233) 812169 or by Pleasurewood Property Sales of Lowestoft, tel. (0502) 500964.

CHAPTER TWENTY EIGHT:
PACKAGED HOLIDAYS IN FRANCE

Although this book is written primarily for the independent traveller visiting the region by car, there are of course many other alternatives.

Coach holidays

Ron and Jenny Farmer, who run Francophiles Discover France, offer Riches of Provence, a two-week holiday usually in May, leaving from Bristol, for about £570 per person, including all travel, half board, a courier and all excursions. All the main Roman sights in Vaison-la-Romaine, Pont-du-Gard, Orange, Nîmes and Arles are visited, as well as the Carmargue. The hotels booked are in Vaison and Anduze (NW of Nîmes). The address is 66 Great Brockeridge, Westbury on Trym, Bristol, BS9 3UA, tel. (0272) 621975.

Savoir France, West Side, North Littleton, Evesham, Worcs. tel. (0386) 832903, also offer two-week coach holidays to Provence.

Slipaway Tours, 90 Newland Road, Worthing, West Sussex, tel. (0903) 213751, have eight-day coach tours to Provence.

Thomas Cook, Club Cantabrica Holidays, Facet Travel and Roman City Tours also have coach holidays.

Art, architecture and history study holidays

A wide variety of 'intellectual' holidays to Provence are available from:

● Ace Study Tours, Babraham, Cambridge CB2 4AP, tel. (0223) 835055.

- Canvas Holidays, Bull Plain, Hertford SG14 1DY, tel. (0992) 553535.
- Facet Travel, Oakwood House, Eastern Road, Wivelsfield Green, Sussex, tel. (0444) 84351.
- Francophiles Discover France, 66 Gt. Brockeridge, Westbury on Trym, Bristol BS9 3UA, tel. (0272) 621975.
- Plantaganet Tours, 85 The Grove, Moordown, Bournemouth BH9 2TY, tel. (0202) 521895.
- Prospect Art Tours, 10 Barley Mow Passage, London W4 4PH, tel. 01-995-2163.
- Association for Active Learning, 9 Haywra Street, Harrogate H61 5BJ, tel. (0423) 525778.
- Callers Pegasus Travel (modern art), 3 Osborne Terrace, Newcastle-on-Tyne, tel, 091 281 4831.
- Page and Moy (Historic Tour), 136–40 London Road, Leicester LE2 1EN, tel. (0533) 552521.
- Serenissima Travel, 21 Dorset Square, London NW1 6DQ, tel. 01-730-9841.
- Swan Hellenic Art Treasures, 77 New Oxford Street, London WC1A 1PP, tel. 01-831-1616.

Traditional crafts

- H.F. Holidays, 142–4 Great North Way, London NW4 1EG, tel. 01-203-1115.

Boat/yacht hire

This is usually for the Camargue.
- French Leave, 21 Fleet Street, London EC4, tel. 01-583-8383.
- Thomas Cook, P.O. Box 36, Peterborough PE3 6SB, tel. (0733) 502200.
- Blakes Holidays, Wroxham, Norwich NR12 8DH, tel. (0605) 33224.
- Slipaway Holidays, 90 Newland Road, Worthing BN11 1LB, tel. (0903) 821000.
- Clearway Holidays, 17 Heath Terrace, Leamington Spa, CV32 5NA, tel. (0926) 450002.

- Crown Cruisers, 8 Ber Street, Norwich NR1 3EJ, tel. (0603) 630513

Music festivals

- G.W. Henebery (Aix music festival), Kareol, Islip, Oxford OX5 2SU, tel. (0867) 56341.

Writing holidays

- Writers in Provence, 6 Rhonda Grove, London E3 5AP offer a writers' course in the Luberon valley, east of Avignon.

Châteaux holidays

- Vacances en Campagne, Bignor, Pulborough, West Sussex, tel. (0798) 7292.
- International Services, 7a Haymarket, London SW1Y 4BU, tel. 01-930-5551.
- Chapter Travel, 126 St Johns Wood High Street, London NW8, tel. 01-586-9451.
- Air France Holidays, 69 Boston Manor Road, Brentford, Middlesex TW8 9JQ, tel. 01-568-6981.
- Allez France, 27 West Street, Storrington, West Sussex RH20 4DZ, tel. (0906) 62345.
- Aries Holidays, 57 Joyce Road, Bungay, Suffolk NR35 1LA, tel. (0986) 5552.
- Billington Travel, 2 White Hart Parade, Riverhead, Sevenoaks, Kent TN13 2BJ, tel. (0732) 460666.

Staying with French families

- Euro Academy Outbound, 77a George Street, Croydon, CR0 1LD, tel. 01-686-2363.
- En Famille Agency, The Old Stable, 60b Maltravers Street, Arundel, BN18 9BG, tel. (0903) 883266.

French language courses

- Euro Academy, 77a George Street, Croydon CR0 1LD, tel. 01-686-2363.

- En Famille Agency, The Old Stable, 60b Maltravers Street, Arundel BN18 9BG, tel. (0903) 883266.
- L.S.G.F., 201 Main Street, Thornton LE6 1AH, tel. (0509) 261205.
- Also at Universities of Aix-en-Provence (2) and Avignon.

Holiday villages

- French Villa Centre, 175 Selsdon Park Road, Croydon CR2 8JJ, tel. 01-651-1231.
- Just France, Eternit House, Felsham Road, London SW15 1SF, tel. 01-788-3878.
- Hoseasons Holidays Abroad, Sunway House, Lowestoft NR32 3LT, tel. (0502) 500555.

Nature studies in the Camargue

- Cygnus Wildlife Holidays, 96 Fore Street, Kingsbridge TQ7 1PY, tel. (0548) 6178.
- Sunsites, Sunsite House, Station Road, Dorking, Surrey RM4 1YZ, tel. (0306) 887733.

Cookery course holidays

- Country Special Tours (for groups only), 153b Kidderminster Road, Bewdley, DY12 1JE, tel. (0299) 403528.

Naturist/nudist holidays

- Peng Travel, 86 Station Road, Gidea Park, Essex RM2 6DB, tel. (0402) 471832.

Cycling holidays

- Susi Madrons 'Cycling for Softies', Lloyds House, 22 Lloyds Street, Manchester, M2 5WA, tel. 061-834-6800.
- Leicester Study Group, 201 Main Street, Thornton LE6 1AH, tel. (0509) 261205.

Painting holidays

- British Airways Holidays, P.O. Box 100, Hodford House, 17/27 High Street, Hounslow TW3 1TB, tel. 01-748-7559.

181

- H.F. Holidays, 142/4 Great North Way, London NW4 1EG, tel. 01-203-0433.

Riding holidays

- Leicester Study Group, 201 Main Street, Thornton LE6 1AH, tel. (0509) 261205.

Pilgrimage tours

- Interchurch Travel, 45 Berkeley Street, London W1X 1PH, tel. 01-734-0942.

Health and fitness holidays

- France Directe, 2 Church Street, Warwick CV34 4AB, tel. (0926) 497989.

Tennis holidays

- Air France Holidays (Arles), 69 Boston Manor Road, Brentford TW8 9JQ, tel. 01-568-6981.
- Sophia Country Club, 1 Choule Gardens, Granby Road, Old Stevenage, Herts. SG1 4BY, tel. (0438) 350274.

Singles holidays

- Solos, 41 Watford Way, London NW4 3JH, tel. 01-202-0855.

Walking/rambling tours

- Ramblers Holidays, Box 43, Welwyn Garden City, Herts. AL8 6PQ, tel. (0707) 331133.
- Waymark Holidays, 295 Lillie Road, London SW6 7LL, tel. 01-385-5015.
- Acorn Venture, 32 Woodland Avenue, West Hagley, Stourbridge DY8 2XQ, tel. (0562) 886569.
- Countrywide Holiday Association, Birch Heys, Cromwell Range, Manchester M14 6HU, tel. 061-225-1000.
- Just France, Eternit House, Felsham Road, London SW15 1SF, tel. 01-788-3878.
- Serenissima Travel, 21 Dorset Square, London NW1 6DQ, tel. 01-730-9841.

- Leicester Study Group, 201 Main Street, Thornton LE6 1AH, tel. (0509) 261205.

Wine tours/tasting holidays to Provence and Rhône Valley

- Country Special Holidays, 153b Kidderminster Road, Bewdley DY12 1JE, tel. (0299) 403578.
- Facet Travel, Oakwood House, Eastern Road, Wivelsfield Green, Sussex, tel. (0444) 84351.
- Just France, Eternit House, Felsham Road, London SW15 1SF, tel. 01-788-3878.
- Moswin Tours, P.O. Box 8, 3 Ashton Close, Oadby, Leicester LE2 5WX, tel. (0533) 719922.
- Slipaway Holidays, 90 Newland Road, Worthing BN11 1LB, tel. (0903) 821000.
- David Walker Travel, 10b Littlegate Street, Oxford OX1 1QT, tel. (0865) 728136.
- World Wine Tours, 4 Dorchester Road, Drayton, St Leonard OX9 8BH, tel. (0865) 891919.
- Francophiles Discover France, 66 Gt. Brockeridge, Westbury on Trym, Bristol, tel. (0272) 621975.
- Country Wide Holidays, Birch Heys, Cromwell Range, Manchester M14 6HU, tel. 061-225-1000.

Camping/caravanning/mobile homes

- A.C.T. Holidays, 17 Chorley Old Road, Bolton BL1 3AD, tel. (0204) 388108.
- Angel Travel, 47 High Street, Central Chambers, Tonbridge, tel. (0732) 361115.
- Canvas Holidays, 9/13 Bull Plain, Hertford SG14 1DY, tel. (0992) 553535
- Carasol Holidays, 6 Hayes Avenue, Bournemouth BH7 7AD, tel. (0202) 33398.
- Carefree Camping Holidays, 41–3 Stephyns Chambers, Bank Court, Hemel Hempstead, tel. (0442) 48101.
- Club Cantabrica Holidays, 146–8 London Road, St Albans AL1 1PQ, tel. (0727) 66177.
- Eurocamp Travel, Edmundson House, Tatton Street, Knutsford, WA16 6BG, tel. (0565) 3844.

- French Riviera Holidays, 296 Frome Road, Trowbridge BA14 0DT, tel. (0221) 464040.
- NAT Holidays, Holiday House, Domestic Road, Leeds LS12 6HR, tel. (0532) 434077.
- Rendezvous France, 146–8 London Road, St Albans, Herts AL1 1PG, tel. (0727) 45400.
- Riviera Sailing, 45 Bath Road, Emsworth PO10 7ER, tel. (0243) 374376.
- Seasun Holidays, 83 Station Road, Forest Hall, Newcastle-upon-Tyne, tel. 091-270-0707.
- Selection Holidays, 26 Downsway, Shoreham-by-Sea BN4 5GN, tel. (0273) 461153.
- Sunscene Holidays, 40 Market Place South, Leicester LE1 5HB, tel. (0533) 20644.
- Tentrek Holidays, 152 Maidstone Road, Ruxley Corner, Sidcup DA14 5HS, tel. 01-302-6426.

Camargue

- Page and Moy (Historic Tour), 136–40 London Road, Leicester LE2 1EN, tel. (0533) 552521.
- Roman City Holidays, Bus & Coach Station, Manvers Street, Bath BA1 1JJ, tel. (0225) 445555.
- Andrew Brook, Barley Mow Workspace, 10 Barley Mow Passage, Chiswick W4 4PH, tel. 01-995-3642.
- Martin Sturge, 3 Lower Camden Place, Bath BA1 5JJ, tel. (0225) 310623.

Activity Holidays

- La France des Villages, Model Farm, Rattlesden, Bury St Edmunds IP30 0SY, tel. (0449) 37664.
- Waymark Holidays, 295 Lillie Road, London SW6 7LL, tel. 01-385-5015.
- Canvas Holidays, 9/13 Bull Plain, Hertford SG14 1DY, tel. (0992) 553535.
- Cresta Holidays, 32 Victoria Street, Altrincham WA14 1ET, tel. (0345) 056511.

Youth travel

- Schools Abroad, Grosvenor Hall, Bolnore Road, Haywards Heath, West Sussex, tel. (0444) 414122.

Villa and gîte rentals

- Just France, Eternit House, Felsham Road, London SW15 1SF, tel. 01-788-3878.
- Dominiques Villas, 2 Peterborough Mews, London SW6 3BL, tel. 01-736-1664.
- Allez France, Storrington RH20 4DZ, tel. (0906) 62345.
- V.F.B. Holidays, Cheltenham, Glos. GL50 4DT, tel. (0242) 580187.
- Chapter Travel, 126 St Johns Wood High Street, London NW8, tel. 01-586-9451.
- S.B.H. France, Lavalier House, Tangmere, Chichester, W. Sussex, tel. (0243) 773345.
- La France des Villages, Model Farm, Rattlesden, Bury St Edmunds IP30 0SY, tel. (0898) 900900.
- Kingsland Holidays, 1 Pounds Park Road, Plymouth PL3 4QP, tel. (0752) 766822.
- Cresta Holidays, Victoria Street, Altrincham, WA14 1ET, tel. (0345) 056511.
- Pleasurewood, 107 Somerset House, Lowestoft, Suffolk NR32 1PZ, tel. (0502) 517211.
- Sunvista Holidays, 5a George Street, Warminster, Wiltshire BA12 8QA, tel. (0985) 217444
- Rendezvous France, Holiday House, 146–8 Reading Road, St Albans, AL1 1PQ, tel. (0727) 45400.

Bicycles

These can be rented at the local SCNF rail stations at Arles, Avignon, Bonnières, Isle Fontaine-de-Vaucluse and Nîmes.

UK tour companies offering packages based on local towns

Aix-en-Provence

- Air France Holidays, 69 Boston Manor Road, Brentford, Middx. TW8 9JQ, tel. 01-568-6981.

- Billington Travel, 2a White Hart Parade, Riverhead, Sevenoaks TN13 2BJ, tel. (0732) 460666
- France Directe, 2 Church Street, Warwick CV34 4AB, tel. (0926) 497989.
- French Travel Service, Georgian House, 69 Boston Manor Road, Brentford TW8 0JQ, tel. 01-568-8442.
- France Voyages, 145 Oxford Street, London W1R 1TB, tel. 01-494-3155.
- Lagrange Vacances, 16/20 New Broadway, Ealing, London W5 2XA, tel. 01-579-7311.

Arles
- Air France Holidays, 69 Boston Manor Road, Brentford, Middx. TW8 9JQ, tel. 01-568-6981.
- Billington Travel, 2a White Hart Parade, Riverhead, Sevenoaks TN13 2BJ, tel. (0732) 460666.
- Car Holidays Abroad, Bull Plain, Hertford SG14 1DY, tel. (0992) 551931.
- Cresta Holidays, 6 Acre House, Town Square, Sale M33 1SN, tel. (0345) 056511.
- French Travel Service, Georgian House, 69 Boston Manor Road, Brentford TW8 0JQ, tel. 01-568-8442.
- Just France, Eternit House, Felsham Road, London SW15 1SF, tel. 01-788-3878.

Avignon
- Billington Travel, 2a White Hart Parade, Riverhead, Sevenoaks TN13 2BJ, tel. (0732) 460666.
- David Walker Travel, 10b Littlegate Street, Oxford OX1 1QT, tel. (0865) 728136.
- Quo Vadis, 243 Euston Road, London NW1 2BT, tel. 01-583-8383.

Les Baux
- V.F.B. Holidays, 1 St Margaret's Terrace, Cheltenham, Glos. tel. (0242) 526338.

Carpentras
- Slipaway Holidays, 90 Newland Road, Worthing BN11 1LB, tel. (0903) 821000.

Cassis
- France Directe, 2 Church Street, Warwick CV34 4AB, tel. (0926) 497989.
- Air France Holidays, 69 Boston Manor Road, Brentford, Middx. TW8 9JQ, tel. 01-568-6981.
- France Voyages, 145 Oxford Street, London W1R 1TB, tel. 01-494-3155.

Châteauneuf-du-Pape
- Just France, Eternit House, Felsham Road, London SW15 1SF, tel. 01-788-3878.

La Ciotat
- Euro Express, 227 Shepherds Bush Road, London W6 7AS, tel. 01-748-2607.

Gigondas
- V.F.B. Holidays, 1 St Margaret's Terrace, Cheltenham, Glos., tel. (0242) 526338.

Marseille
- Air France Holidays, 69 Boston Manor Road, Brentford, Middx. TW8 9JQ, tel. 01-568-6981.
- Hamilton Travel, 3 Heddon Street, London W1R 7LE, tel. 01-437-4627.
- Travellers, P.O. Box 379, London, E9 6JR, tel. 01-533-2486.

St Rémy-de-Provence
- France Directe, 2 Channel Street, Warwick, CV34 4AB, tel. (0926) 497989.
- Ramblers Holidays, Box 43, Welwyn Garden City, Herts. AL8 6PQ, tel. (0707) 331133.

Tavel
● V.F.B. Holidays, 1 St Margaret's Terrace, Cheltenham, Glos. tel. (0242) 526338.

Air Flights to Marseille	Air France
	British Airways
Flights within France	Air Inter
French rail bookings	SNCF, 179 Piccadilly, London W1V 0BA, tel. 01-493-9731
Regular bus/coach services	International Express/Eurolines have services to Aix-en-Provence, Avignon, Marseille and Nîmes — from London, 13 Regent Street SW1Y 4UR, tel. 01-439-9368

Local cultural tours

● Loisirs Acceuil, based in the Arles Tourist Office, 35 Place de la République, 13200 Arles, offer a wide range of Van Gogh tours (1989 was his centenary year).
● Association Heliante, Mas du Retiras, 13520 Les Baux-de-Provence, offer seven- or ten-day painting courses in the places where Van Gogh painted.
● The Centre Franco-Americain, 23 Bd. de la République, 84000 Avignon, offer two-, three- or four-week French language courses in private home accommodation.
● Rouvet, 140 Ave. Général de Gaulle, 84100 Orange, offer a six-day Painters of Provence tour, including two days in Arles.
● Orvac, 6 Place des Marseillaises, 13001 Marseille, offer a wide range of tours within Provence and the Camargue (preferably groups).

CHAPTER TWENTY NINE: REGIONAL RECIPES

SARDINES FARCIES AUX ÉPINARDS
Sardines stuffed with spinach

This recipe is best suited to a rich fish like herring or mackerel, though sea bass or trout can also be used. It is superb with salmon, which gives a contrast of colour as well as taste.

Serves 6

0.75–1 kg	fresh sardines	1½–2 lb
	salt and pepper	
750 g	fresh spinach	1½ lb
	3 Tbsp olive oil	
	1 onion, finely chopped	
	1 Tbsp flour	
185 ml	milk	6 fl oz
	2 cloves garlic, chopped	
	pinch of grated nutmeg	
30 g	dry breadcrumbs	1 oz

Slit the stomach opening of each sardine slightly to clean it. Slit each sardine along each side of the backbone to free it. Continue to separate the fillet meat from the bone, until you reach the stomach. With scissors, cut through the backbone at the head and tail and pull out the bone, leaving head and tail attached, so the fish looks whole. Wipe off the scales and dry each sardine. Sprinkle the sardines with salt and pepper.

Remove the stems from the spinach and wash the leaves thoroughly. Cook the spinach in a large pot of boiling salted water for 5 minutes or until just tender. Drain, rinse under cold

189

running water and drain thoroughly, squeezing to remove as much water as possible. Finely chop the spinach. Set the oven at very hot (220°C/425°F).

Heat half the oil in a saucepan, add the onion and cook over a low fire, stirring often, until soft but not brown. Add the spinach and cook over a medium fire, for a few minutes or until most moisture has evaporated. Sprinkle with the flour and stir over a low fire for 1–2 minutes. Add the milk, garlic, salt, pepper and nutmeg. Bring to a boil, stirring, and simmer for 3–4 minutes; taste for seasoning.

Stuff each sardine with a small spoonful of the spinach mixture. Spoon the remaining spinach mixture into a large oiled baking dish and lay the sardines on top. Sprinkle with breadcrumbs, then with the remaining oil. Bake in the oven for 10 minutes or until golden brown and just tender. Serve in the baking dish.

RAGOÛT AUX ARTICHAUTS
Mutton and artichoke stew

Most traditional Provençal recipes call for mutton, not lamb, as the sheep were raised for wool rather than for meat. Sheep rearing is one of the most ancient Provençal occupations and in the old days the shepherd was a popular figure, carrying news from village to village as he drove his flock to and from the summer pastures, high in the foothills of the Alps. Today's twice-yearly migration is more mundane, taking place by truck.

Serves 6

2 kg	breast or shoulder of mutton or lamb	4½ lb
	2 Tbsp oil	
750 g	onions, sliced	1½ lb
	1 Tbsp flour	
185 ml	white wine	6 fl oz
400 ml	broth	¾ pt
	2 cloves garlic, crushed	
	1 large tomato, quartered	
	bouquet garni	
	salt and pepper	

12 small OR 6 medium artichokes
juice of ½ lemon

Trim off the excess fat; cut breast in sections or shoulder in 5 cm/2 in chunks. Heat the oil in a heavy based casserole, add the meat and brown it well on all sides over a fairly high fire. Remove the meat, add the onions and cook over a low fire, stirring often, for 10 minutes or until soft but not brown. Sprinkle the onions with the flour and continue to cook for 2–3 minutes or until brown, stir in the wine and the broth, return the meat to the casserole and add the garlic, tomato, bouquet garni, salt and pepper. Bring to a boil, cover and simmer for 1 hour.

While the meat is simmering, prepare the artichokes: remove the stems and break off the tough leaves. Cut tops off the other leaves to within 2–5 cm/1 in of the artichoke bottoms. Quarter the artichokes lengthwise and remove the chokes with a spoon; cut medium artichokes in eight. Drop artichokes into a bowl of water and add lemon juice.

Drain the artichokes, add them to the meat and simmer for another 30 minutes or until the meat and artichokes are tender. Skim off the excess fat and discard the bouquet garni; taste for seasoning. Serve from the casserole.

RATATOUILLE

'Ratatouille' is among the many names that linger from the old Provençal language. Two teaspoons of the herb mixture 'herbes de Provence' may be substituted for the basil, thyme and aniseed in the recipe.

Serves 4

	1 medium aubergine, halved and cut	
	in 1 cm/⅜in slices	
350 g	**small courgettes, cut in 1.25 cm/½ in slices**	¾ lb
	salt and pepper	
60 ml	**olive oil**	2 fl oz
	2 medium onions, thinly sliced	
500 g	**tomatoes, peeled, seeded and chopped**	1 lb
	2 red or green peppers, cored, seeded and sliced	

> **2 cloves garlic, crushed**
> **1 tsp basil**
> **½ tsp thyme**
> **½ tsp ground coriander**
> **a pinch of crushed aniseed**
> **1 Tbsp chopped parsley (for sprinkling)**

Sprinkle the aubergine/eggplant and courgette/zucchini slices with salt and let stand for 30 minutes to draw out their liquid. Drain them, rinse with cold water and dry on paper towels.

Heat half the oil in a large casserole, add the onions and cook over low heat, occasionally stirring, until soft but not brown. Layer the onions, aubergine, courgettes, tomatoes and peppers in the casserole, sprinkling the garlic, herbs, salt and pepper between the layers. Spoon the remaining oil on top. Cover and simmer for 30–40 minutes or until all of the vegetables are just tender; if overcooked, they become soft and watery. If the vegetables do produce a great deal of liquid, remove the lid for the last 15 minutes of cooking. Taste for seasoning.

Either serve the ratatouille from the casserole or transfer it to a serving dish. Sprinkle with parsley and serve hot or at room temperature.

PISTOU
Basil, parmesan and garlic sauce

'Pistou' has many uses: it can be served as a sauce for spaghetti or mixed into vegetable soup to make 'soupe au pistou'. It is an excellent dip for raw vegetables and in the Nice area pistou is also served with roast mutton.

Makes 185 ml/6 fl oz of sauce

	10 basil leaves	
	3 large cloves garlic	
100 g	**freshly grated parmesan cheese**	**3½ oz**
80 ml	**olive oil**	**3 fl oz**

Wash the basil leaves and dry them as thoroughly as possible. Crush the garlic in a mortar with a pestle until it becomes a paste; then add the basil and again pound to a fine paste.

Transfer to a bowl. Gradually add the grated cheese, mixing and mashing with a fork. Still using a fork, gradually stir in the olive oil, drop by drop, so the sauce thickens; if the oil is added too quickly, the mixture may separate. Alternatively, make the sauce in a food processor or blender: purée the basil, garlic and cheese; then add the oil gradually, with the blades turning.

To keep pistou for use in the winter, put it in a glass jar and run a thin layer of olive oil on top to keep out the air. Cover the jar tightly and keep it in a cool dry place.

SPAGHETTI AU PISTOU
For 4 servings, cook:

250 g   **spaghetti**   ½ lb

and drain. Toss it in a little olive oil; then add the pistou. Season with salt and pepper to taste. Serve more grated parmesan cheese separately.

INDEX